COYOTE PETERSON

THE KING OF STING

Little, Brown and Company
New York Boston

Cover design by Ching N. Chan. Cover illustrations by Johanna Tarkela.
Cover photography by Chris Casella.
Contributions by Daniel Chance Ross.

All pages: © Nella/shutterstock.com

Front matter: © fotoslaz/shutterstock.com; © Mariyana M/shutterstock.com | **The Climb Begins…:**
© Denisse Leon/shutterstock.com; © Michiel de Wit/shutterstock.com; © kunchit jantana/shutterstock.com;
© Mariyana M/shutterstock.com | **Chapter 1:** © Janice Adlam/shutterstock.com; © Anton-Burakov/shutterstock.com;
© Grobler du Preez/shutterstock.com; © Bardocz Peter/shutterstock.com; © VectorPot/shutterstock.com |
Chapter 2: © Le Do/shutterstock.com; © Bardocz Peter/shutterstock.com; © fotoslaz/shutterstock.com;
© Mariyana M/shutterstock.com; © Susan Schmitz/shutterstock.com; © VectorPot/shutterstock.com |
Chapter 3: © Denisse Leon/shutterstock.com; © Bardocz Peter/shutterstock.com; © fotoslaz/shutterstock.com;
© VectorPot/shutterstock.com | **Chapter 4:** © AlexussK/shutterstock.com; © Bardocz Peter/shutterstock.com;
© VectorPot/shutterstock.com | **Chapter 5:** © Anton-Burakov/shutterstock.com; © Bardocz Peter/shutterstock.com;
© Melinda Fawver/shutterstock.com; © VectorPot/shutterstock.com | **Chapter 6:** © Denisse Leon/
shutterstock.com; © fotoslaz/shutterstock.com; © Mariyana M/shutterstock.com; © VectorPot/shutterstock.com |
Chapter 7: © Le Do/shutterstock.com; © Denisse Leon/shutterstock.com; © Nik Merkulov/shutterstock.com;
© Bardocz Peter/shutterstock.com; © VectorPot/shutterstock.com | **Chapter 8:** © Anton-Burakov/shutterstock.com;
© Bardocz Peter/shutterstock.com; © VectorPot/shutterstock.com; © Daniel Prudek/shutterstock.com;
© StockMediaSeller/shutterstock.com | **Chapter 9:** © mikeledra/shutterstock.com; © Chansom Pantip/
shutterstock.com; © Bardocz Peter/shutterstock.com; © VectorPot/shutterstock.com | **Chapter 10:** © Chansom Pantip/
shutterstock.com; © Bardocz Peter/shutterstock.com; © VectorPot/shutterstock.com | **Chapter 11:** © Bardocz Peter/
shutterstock.com; © VectorPot/shutterstock.com

Little, Brown and Company
Hachette Book Group
1290 Avenue of the Americas, New York, NY 10104
Visit us at LBYR.com
bravewilderness.com

First Edition: November 2018

Little, Brown and Company is a division of Hachette Book Group, Inc.
The Little, Brown name and logo are trademarks of Hachette Book Group, Inc.

The publisher is not responsible for websites (or their content) that are not owned by the publisher.

Library of Congress Control Number 2018956523

ISBNs: 978-0-316-45238-0 (paper over board), 978-0-316-45371-4 (ebook),
978-0-316-42314-4 (ebook), 978-0-316-45373-8 (ebook)

Printed in the United States of America

LSC-C

10 9 8 7 6 5 4 3 2 1

**Disclaimer: Coyote Peterson and the crew are professionally
trained and receive assistance from animal experts when in
potentially life-threatening situations. Never approach or
attempt to handle wildlife on your own.**

Contents

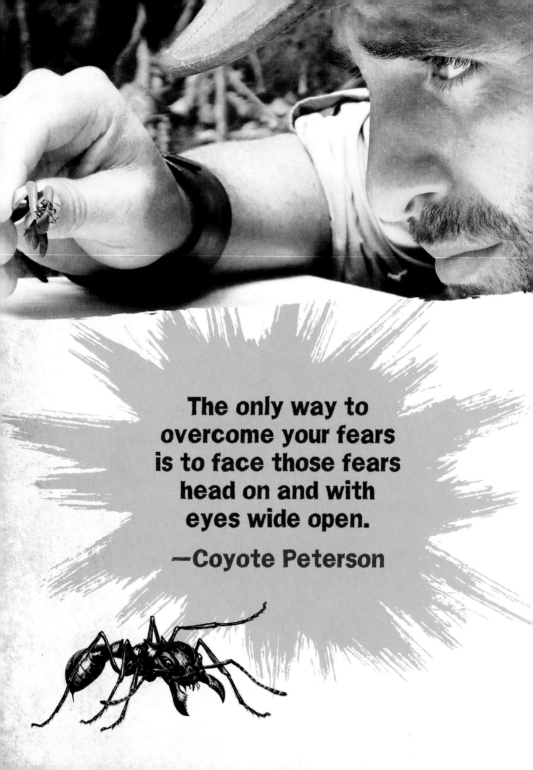

The only way to overcome your fears is to face those fears head on and with eyes wide open.

—Coyote Peterson

THE CLIMB BEGINS...

**My name is Coyote Peterson, and
I'm about to enter the Sting Zone!**

If you're reading this book, chances are you've heard me say that sentence—or one close to it, with *bite* or *strike* rather than *sting*—more times than you probably realize. In the past four years, it's become my rallying cry to the Coyote Pack (that's all of you!) as I've embarked upon some of the most daring and painful animal encounters of my life.

Since I first launched my YouTube channel, Brave Wilderness, on September 14, 2014, my fearless crew and I have filmed many thrilling interactions with all kinds of bizarre or misunderstood species.

I've gone headfirst into leech-infested swamps searching for prehistoric-looking snapping turtles, pressed far into the backcountry of Alaska to track down beautiful sockeye salmon, and even traveled to Australia, where I got hands-on with agile monitor lizards. I've also worked with some of the cutest, cuddliest, most adorable animals in the world, from pine martens and koalas, to baby reindeer and three-toed sloths, who did NOT bite or sting me.

Then there are the episodes that are strongly based on conservation, like the time I worked alongside a field veterinarian team on a South African game reserve, where we successfully tranquilized, got up close to, and collected biometric data from a pride of lions.

Our videos on the Brave Wilderness channel have captured the world's attention and ignited a new generation's love for animals. My fearless team and I have successfully built the world's largest animal adventure brand in the digital space and have captivated millions and millions of inquisitive minds

in the process. We've garnered the attention of kids, their parents, and even their grandparents as we created excitement around a plethora of creatures they otherwise may have known nothing about.

About a year after Brave Wilderness launched, I stumbled into what's become my most daring—and, unfortunately for me, painful—set of adventures: getting stung by the world's most terrifying insects. From a red-hot mound of fire ants in South Florida, to a giant wasp called the tarantula hawk in Arizona's Sonoran Desert, to what was rumored to be the most potent sting in the world—the massive bullet ant, found in the rain forests of Costa Rica—I've endured levels of pain that are almost unimaginable. But for me this journey hasn't been about trying to look like a tough guy because, truth be told, I'm not one and I've never been one. It also wasn't about getting millions of views on YouTube or becoming famous. I became the center of this crazy human experiment so I could teach the world about these creepy-looking insects that they would have otherwise feared.

I *love* animals, and ever since I was a kid chasing snapping turtles in the swamps behind my family's house in Ohio, I've been fascinated with the bizarre, the dangerous, and the unknowns of the animal kingdom. I grew up with role models like the late great Crocodile Hunter, Steve Irwin, and I always hoped that one day I could become a role model myself. I wanted nothing more than to teach the world about conservation, humans' impact on animal habitats, and ways we can give our animal friends the kind of love and respect they deserve. Today, I am fortunate to be in that position, and I couldn't be more grateful.

But when people think about the importance of caring for and protecting animals, they don't often consider insects. They might scream, "What's that horrible creepy-crawly thing in my house?" before crushing a harmless praying mantis with their shoe.

With the Brave Wilderness YouTube channel, I've caught some of the world's most feared insects—like the massively intimidating tarantula hawk, a wasp who paralyzes tarantulas with a quarter-inch

stinger—then set these alien-looking creatures on my forearm as my crew filmed them stinging me. Why? To show the audience that insects deserve respect, not fear. Sure, it might be fun to watch me roll around on the ground, screaming in agony and pounding my fists because I feel as if the electrical current of a Taser is shooting up my arm. But at the end of the day, I want people to understand these insects rather than thoughtlessly brushing them aside or aimlessly killing them. They're not menaces to the environment; they're fascinating creatures who play a distinct and incredibly important role within our planet and its ever-evolving ecosystem.

My winding saga through the world of animals has been nothing short of an incredible experience, but like any great journey, my team and I have faced many roadblocks and challenges along the way. This book is my chance to tell all of you—my fearless Coyote Pack—about everything you haven't seen on the screen. I've worked to make *The King of Sting* a fun, accessible combination of science that focuses on the insects in my most clicked-upon sting episodes, mixed with behind-the-scenes insight that pulls back the curtain and reveals what it took to produce them.

You'll see me battle my own fears along this thrilling voyage, you'll come to understand how entomologist Justin Schmidt's insect sting pain index provided a road map for many of the episodes we produced, and you'll meet all the people who stood by me as I got stung by the world's most infamous insects. And best of all, you'll finally see me come forearm-to-stinger with the insect who gave this book its name—the undisputed, one and only King of Sting: **THE EXECUTIONER WASP!**

That's right, folks. I'm not the King of Sting, nor would I ever claim to be, even though the phrase is often connected to the name *Coyote Peterson*. The true king of this story—and of all stinging insects—is the incredibly intimidating wasp that now proudly stands atop the world-renowned insect sting pain index. The insect with the most painfully potent sting on Earth—a sting that literally seared my flesh and melted a crater in my forearm with its highly toxic venom. Trust me, with his yellow-and-red banding, his chomping mandibles, or mouthparts, and his terrifying quarter-inch-long stinger, this creature is a living nightmare. Yet, before we unveil and officially crown the king, we must embark upon a painfully thrilling journey to bring this creature into the spotlight. So, if you're ready for one crazy ride, roll up your sleeves, grab your entomology forceps, and prepare to enter the

Sting Zone!

CHAPTER 1

PORCUPINE
(ERETHIZON DORSATUM)

PAIN INDEX
2

ENTER THE SPIKE ZONE!

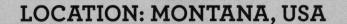

It all started with a porcupine.

In the summer of 2014—before the Brave Wilderness channel launched on YouTube—my producers, director Mark and camera operator Chance; our wildlife biologist, Mario; and I boarded an airplane for the trip of a lifetime: a visit to a wildlife sanctuary located in the heart of the Rocky Mountains in backcountry Bozeman, Montana. Our ultimate goal was to film an incredibly daring encounter in which I would get face-to-face with a 750-pound grizzly bear. This episode was poised to be the centerpiece of the summer we spent filming the first season of *Breaking Trail*, but little did we know that getting pummeled around by this giant apex predator would not be the most famous episode to emerge from this adventure.

When we arrived in Bozeman, we unloaded our filming equipment from the vehicles, hiked into the rugged mountainous terrain, and scouted for an ideal location to begin production. Just so it's clear:

We would be working alongside a bear who had been raised in captivity and not a wild bear. Adam the Grizzly Bear had been featured in countless movies and television commercials, so while this interaction certainly had a threat of danger, Adam was as kindhearted as it got. As most of you know, or have by now seen, the purpose of that episode was to show you what to do if you encounter a bear in the wild. It's certainly a story unto itself, but this chapter is not about bears: It's about where Coyote Peterson—facing down and enduring copious amounts of pain—began.

"Hey, Coyote!" one of the wildlife handlers said after we'd wrapped up filming with Adam. "We've got a young porcupine who was raised here. Do you guys think you might want to film an episode with him as well?"

Now, I'm never one to shy away from the opportunity for an amazing animal encounter. But a porcupine? I saw a dog quilled by one when I was ten years old and traveling through South Dakota with my mom and sister. It was a scene I'll never forget. That poor dog's snout was covered in quills, he couldn't eat, and his eyes were swollen shut! I watched with a vicarious agony, my teeth clenched tight as I saw his owners struggle to forcefully remove the quills. Poor pooch! The whole ordeal traumatized me, and ever since, I have always wished there was a way to help unfortunate animals who get painfully curious about a porcupine.

That's when the little light bulb in my head lit up!

You know what, Coyote? What if a person or their pet got spiked by a porcupine and they had to act fast to remove the quills? How would they know the right way to do it?

My mission on every wildlife encounter I film for Brave Wilderness is to teach people about animals. I want the Coyote Pack to live through my experiences but also come away with new knowledge or a handy skill set. Could the safe removal of porcupine quills be part of that? Why not? Obviously, it would be wrong to film a dog getting quilled, so I hatched a plan and turned to the handlers and my crew.

"What if I acted as the dog—or the Coyote, in this case—and let the porcupine quill *me*?"

Seeing me getting bitten, stung, and spiked—all while learning something from the process—is exactly what the Coyote Pack is hungry for.

QUILLS: needle-sharp modified hairs

GUARD HAIRS: sensory defense system

BACK FEET: five claws

FRONT FEET: four claws

One of the porcupine handlers laughed. "Well, it would hurt a lot," he said, "but it's *your* hand."

Mark, Mario, and Chance thought my idea was a bit crazy but would make a great episode, so we began to conceptualize it. We talked to the experts who worked at the sanctuary and quickly began to learn about porcupines: what they eat, which predators hunt them, and ultimately how their quills work. We not only began to realize what amazing animals they are, but also what a wild adventure it would be if I got spiked by one so we could teach our viewers how to properly remove the quills. But never, not once, did we say to one another: "Millions of people are going to love seeing Coyote Peterson in pain!"

Four epic years later, after that porcupine video

racked up twenty-seven million views, we know the truth: Seeing me getting bitten, stung, and spiked—all while learning something from the process—is exactly what the Coyote Pack is hungry for.

The light, cutting like razors through the branches of the dense Montana pine forests that summer morning, was absolutely beautiful. The dramatic mood was intensified by the lack of clouds and a fine covering of morning haze. It was the kind of day I would have been happy hiking around in, dawn to dusk, but I had a porcupine and his rump of quills to meet.

The porcupine wranglers, as they soon became known to me and the crew, showed up with what looked like a small dog carrier. Yet inside was the quill-covered beast. They placed the carrier down on a large moss-covered log, and as they slowly opened the wire gate, I

took notice of the long leather gloves they wore. This was their only line of defense against any accidental quilling. Most of the handlers had been quilled before; it's a lesson they say you learn once, and they certainly didn't want it to happen again.

As I looked on expectantly, the little spiker, who seemed to be about fifteen pounds, slowly waddled out and onto the log. Like all North American porcupines, he loved to dig through the brush looking for roots and berries, or scale up pine trees using his textured, pebbly feet and large, pointed claws. The handlers had also told me that sometimes he'd get so excited by the sight of bright-green buds at the end of branches that he'd fall out of a tree, landing—*thump!*—right on the ground.

Like all North American porcupines, he loves to dig through the brush, looking for roots and berries, or scale up pine trees using his textured, pebbly feet and large, pointed claws.

His guard hairs were dark brown and interspersed with sharp white quills, and he had a small, narrow face and round, beady eyes. Most people don't realize that the North American porcupine is the second-largest rodent on this continent, second only to the beaver, but this guy was considered small, a subadult—about the size of a West Highland white terrier. It's still amazing to me that the porcupine is a rodent because rodents encompass such a diverse spread, from beavers to mice to rats to muskrats. And then there's the porcupine, who really doesn't look like a beaver or rat at all. Instead, with its long claws, round belly, and pointed nose, it's a hybrid of all these different creatures.

"He's not going to run away, is he?" I asked, backing up because I wasn't sure how close I should get to him.

"No way," one of the handlers said. "This porcupine's great. He loves us."

I'm not sure *love* was the right word for him, though. As the little guy stuck his nose in the air to explore his environment, he turned his butt in my direction, taking no interest in me whatsoever.

His claws are perfect for foraging and climbing.

Porcupines aren't outwardly aggressive animals. Though most people shy away from them for fear of getting spiked, there's really no way they'll quill you unless you threaten them. Contrary to popular belief (and a handful of misleading cartoons), porcupines don't shoot out their quills; you have to agitate their guard hairs for the spikes to be thrust into an attacker and subsequently released. Quills come out reflexively, like when your lower leg shoots forward after a doctor taps on your knee with a rubber mallet.

Who would have guessed this porcupine was a fierce animal, though? He was adorable, round, cuddly, and happy as he could be, just moseying around on the log and munching on a leaf the handlers had offered him. Other than his sharp quills, the only parts of him that seemed even remotely intimidating were his narrow, razor-sharp, curved claws, and there were four of them on his front feet and five on his back—but those are used for climbing and digging, not attacking.

I was still a little timid, though. In 2014, I wasn't the Coyote Peterson who'd endured the bites of snapping turtles and alligators or the stings of countless ants, bees, wasps, and scorpions. Let alone come arm-to-stinger with the one and only Executioner wasp. I was a young filmmaker who just wanted to put up a few cool wildlife videos on YouTube. You probably can't see how unsure of myself I was in the video, but my nerves were thrust into overdrive. For encouragement and guidance, I turned to a wrangler for a little advice. His response, with a mischievous smile on his face, was simple and to the point.

"Just brush the back of your hand against his guard hairs, right near the rump," he told me. "And he'll spike you as soon as he realizes you're not going away." So I did just that.

I cautiously inched my hand forward and gently brushed the guard hairs. The porcupine didn't register me at first. He kept shifting back and forth, as if he were trying to avoid me. When I touched him again, he

Hey! Coyote! Don't touch my butt!

moved more, shimmying his rear as if he were saying to me, *Hey! Coyote! Don't touch my butt!* Then, on my third attempt, he thrust his rump up with authority and struck my hand with an alarming amount of power.

Whoosh! With lightning-fast speed, about thirty quills broke through the skin and buried themselves in my hand. The strike was so fast I didn't even see it. The force—which I'd compare to a car door slamming shut on your hand—jolted my body backward and shot my hand upward.

Aww, that hurts! I said to myself, as much in shock as I was in pain.

I instantly felt a dull numbness in the back of my hand. But this unexpected sensation wasn't from the quills themselves. Unlike stingers, there's no venom in quills, so I wasn't being envenomated. Instead my hand was in shock; the traumatic impact had deadened it for a brief moment.

That sure was a lot of force for an animal so cute and small! I thought.

Meanwhile, the porcupine went about his business, his butt facing me as he shimmied toward another leaf to nibble on.

North American porcupine quills are one to four inches in length, and they're hollow on the inside, so there's not much weight to them. They're notoriously difficult to extract because the ends are barbed, with sharp, protruding bits that face backward, like those you'd find on a fishhook. The barbs are the most dangerous part of the quill itself, and after they are embedded in the curious victim or attacker, they slowly work their way deeper into the quilled area. Then they begin to swell.

Porcupine quills have killed all kinds of animals— from household pets like dogs to predators like coyotes and even grizzly bears—but it's not the force of the quilling that leads to death. Instead, animals can't get the barbed quills out, and their bodies become infected at the site of the punctures, where the quills brought in dirt, oils, pollutants, or anything else that was sitting on the porcupine's body.

PORCUPINE QUILLS

If left untreated, that infection can prove fatal. In fact, hunters have actually stumbled upon skeletons from animals such as bears, wolves, and mountain lions in the woods, perfectly decomposed, with piles of quills littering the forest floor around their skulls. It's simply amazing to me that an animal as small as a porcupine could kill such massive predators.

DID YOU KNOW?

North American porcupine quills can grow up to four inches long and as wide as an eighteen-gauge needle!

As I mentioned, we were filming on a perfectly gorgeous Montana day, but the sun streaming through the trees cast a lot of shadows on the porcupine and the log—and me—so the production quality of the episode was proving to be terrible. The porcupine was dark brown with specks of white, so he blended into the shadows, and half the time, I was totally silhouetted. Plus, the little spiker had refused to sit still during the filming. One of his favorite things to do was turn his rear end toward the camera—I swear he knew exactly what he was doing, and boy, was it frustrating! In short, we'd struggled filming this episode right up to the point when he embedded his quills in my Coyote paw.

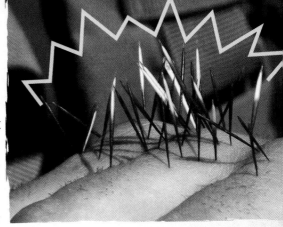

"It's been nice meeting you, porcupine," I said to him, "but it's time for you to go back home to your enclosure and for us to move where the light is better for filming."

Unfortunately, the spot we'd set up to film me removing the quills was about fifteen minutes away—accessible only by foot—so I had to trek with thirty quills in my hand, each one burrowing deeper and causing me more and more pain. The two quills that had landed at the base of my middle finger had struck a nerve, and my hand had seized up, with my fingers spaced apart and bent forward like claws. In fact, my middle finger was completely paralyzed! While I was walking, I had to be careful not to jostle around too much because if I did, the barbs would cut deeper into my flesh, and a burning ache would move through my hand and up my arm. To top it off, I could see that the skin around the embedded quills had started to swell, and I was worried that an infection might soon begin to set in.

In an ideal situation, a person should always seek

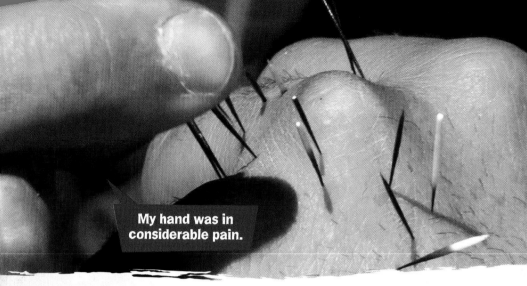

My hand was in considerable pain.

professional medical advice before removing quills
from themselves or their pet—it's always best to have
a doctor or veterinarian do it. However, if you are
deep in the backcountry and need to perform a quill
removal on yourself or a pet, there is a right way and a
wrong way to do it. Our goal was to show you the right
way, so we'd come prepared. We located a meadow
with plenty of sunlight, and I struggled with a single
hand to remove a multi-tool from my belt. This device
had wire snips, which were perfect for performing the
task at hand, and we put them to work immediately.

When a porcupine thrusts its rump, the energy
and force cause the quills to swell, so when they
enter the snout of an attacker—or a hand, in the
case of a human—that swelling causes the barbs to
protrude outward and lock into place. My hand was in
considerable pain at this time, and the irritation was
quickly intensifying, so the first thing I needed to do

was release the pressure inside the quills. To do this, I needed to cut off their tops immediately. This releases trapped air and relaxes the barbs holding the quills in place. I couldn't feel any kind of pressure relief when I finished snipping—like a balloon deflating or a can of fizzy soda opening—nor was there any sound like *whoosh!* on or under the surface of my skin. The depressurization inside the tiny quill is just too subtle to hear or feel, but is crucial to the safe removal of the embedded quills.

Most people's impulse if they get quilled—or if they see their beloved pet yelping in pain with three-inch spikes in their snout—is to yank them out. But I'd talked extensively with the wranglers about the proper way to remove these painful invaders. I knew that, if you have barbs digging into your flesh, pulling on them is only going to rip up your skin more. That, or the barbs will break off inside the wound and will speed up an infection setting in. When the quill is at ease after you snip its tip, the barbs relax and become pliable. If you twist the quills to the side, the barbs relax further. Then, *presto!* You can remove them

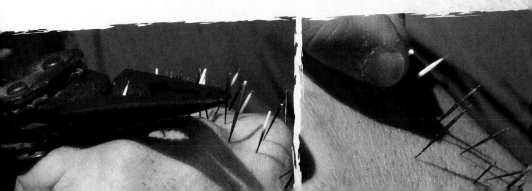

safely. Best of all, there won't be any sharp, prickly fragments left inside your skin to cause a lasting and painful infection.

Whoa! This feels crazy! I thought to myself as I carefully grasped each quill, twisted, and pulled. *It's like someone coated them in Vaseline, because they're*

Whoa! This feels crazy!

sliding right out! There was no ripping, just a smooth, gentle motion as I pulled each quill from my flesh. I can't really explain why the quills felt lubricated— they weren't—so I can only assume that I'd done a really good job turning them ever so slightly to the side, causing them to spiral and slide free without breaking inside.

Finally, I arrived at the two quills in my middle finger, and man, they felt awful!

"*Aww*, jeez, that hurts!" I screamed as I used the mini-tool to extract them slowly and carefully. I winced as blood seeped up through the quill holes, and then exhaled a sigh of relief when it was finally over. I was free of the porcupine's quills!

When I think about it now, I was lucky to have been quilled

by a North American porcupine as opposed to another species such as the Cape porcupine. Also called the South African porcupine, which is found—you guessed it—in South Africa, this variety has quills so long and rigid they can go right through a person's hand and out the other side. North American porcupine quills are considerably smaller than the South African quills, so I'd say I chose wisely in my quill selection for filming this episode.

The South African porcupine has quills so long and rigid they can go right through a person's hand and out the other side.

I was also smart not to engage with a truly defensive porcupine, like one who's at threat of being eaten by a grizzly bear. A porcupine who is being considered for a meal is thinking, *If that bear flips me on my back, he's going to expose my belly, and I'm going to be lunch!* So to defend itself, the porcupine will turn his rear feet backward (yes, North American porcupines can do that) and shimmy in any direction necessary to hold off an attack. Porcupines are slow animals, and it's impossible for even a relatively fast human to outrun a bear, so a porcupine will become extra aggressive when threatened by a predator.

The animal's only hope is turning up its rump in a

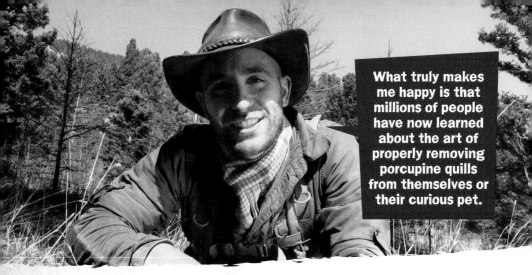

What truly makes me happy is that millions of people have now learned about the art of properly removing porcupine quills from themselves or their curious pet.

rush of porcupine adrenaline, then whacking the bear with its quills—*hard*. Again, a porcupine won't shoot its quills, but they will definitely come out of its body with great force and will certainly send that bear running in the opposite direction with a snout full of agony.

By the time I extracted all the quills, which really only took about ten minutes, my paralyzed claw-hand had returned to normal. It then took a full forty-eight hours after the ordeal for the swelling to completely diminish at the site of the punctures, and the best news of all was that absolutely no infection had formed!

In the end, was it worth it? I'd definitely say *yes!* Because at the moment of this writing, my painful porcupine quilling episode is the most-watched porcupine video in the world. It has over twenty-eight million views, which amazes me for an episode that had been planned at the last minute and experienced so many production issues. However, it's not the millions of views I am excited about; what truly makes me happy is that millions of people have now learned about the art of properly removing porcupine quills from themselves or their curious pet.

After the success of this video, Mark, Chance, Mario, and I realized we could educate our viewers about animals with a slightly different slant, one that would put me in the experimental seat so the audience could learn firsthand from my experiences. The porcupine was just the beginning.

The Brave Wilderness team was onto something! Coyote Peterson was going to have to embark on a new challenge to educate his viewers and let them live vicariously through his pain.

And while we didn't know it yet...a world of stinging insects was calling!

CHAPTER 2

SCORPION
(HADRURUS ARIZONENSIS)

PAIN INDEX
2

THE SCORPION STING ZONE!

LOCATION: ARIZONA, USA

I've said it time and time again: Facing your fears often leads to life's most epic adventures. Even more important, it might teach you something that will help change the way you look at the natural world, especially when it comes to animals.

Four years ago, there was nothing that made my skin crawl more than scorpions. With their outsize lobster-like pincers, chomping mandibles, and venomous, quick-striking stingers, even thinking about scorpions sent chills up my spine. But if I wanted to teach the Coyote Pack about the importance of confronting something that scares you, I knew I had to film myself getting stung by one.

I've had a fear of scorpions since I was a kid. My mom, my sister, and I used to travel across the United States during the summer months, exploring forested national parks in the Midwest, flat wheat-covered plains in middle America, and the vast, sprawling deserts that cover the Southwest. I always loved the quiet beauty of the desert, but if I saw a scorpion scuttling along the ground, looking for a cool, shady rock to hide under, I'd jump up and run in the opposite direction. *That thing is terrifying!* I'd think. *I'd better get out of here before it stings me!*

In the summer of 2014, the Brave Wilderness crew and I headed out to the Sonoran Desert in Arizona, trekking almost an hour outside of the city of Tucson. Our intention was simple: We wanted to film an episode that would educate our viewers about scorpion stings. We would show them that this scary-looking creature should be respected, not killed out of fear. If Coyote Peterson— someone who'd hated scorpions his entire life—could demonstrate that a sting didn't hurt all that much, maybe we could save the lives of scorpions everywhere.

During the day, the sky is a bright-blue, cloudless vista, and at night pinpricks of stars extend as far as the eye can see. The Sonoran Desert is a massive, rugged expanse, and its animals, such as rattlesnakes, Gila monsters, coyotes, kangaroo rats, javelinas, and more, roam freely through it.

There are also scorpions—millions and millions of venomous scorpions.

SONORAN DESERT

One morning over breakfast, after we'd spent a productive few days filming episodes with several of these desert creatures, we realized that scorpions seemed to be around every turn. And I was nervous about each and every one of them. They were nearly impossible to avoid, and we began discussing how painful a sting must be, because none of us had ever actually been stung.

"Maybe you should take a sting so we can all find out," said Mark with a laugh in his voice. "You ready for this one, Coyote?"

No, I was not! I was paralyzed with fear. Sure, I'd been scraped up by the razor-sharp claws of a snapping turtle and quilled by a porcupine, but I hadn't been stung by anything except a honey bee in years.

That thing is terrifying! I'd better get out of here before it stings me!

"I—I don't think this is a good idea," I stammered. "What if I have an allergic reaction and have to go to the hospital?"

"Nah, it won't be that bad!" chimed in Mario. "We can use a giant desert hairy scorpion for the sting. It won't be any worse than a bee sting."

Easy for him to say—he wouldn't be the one going hand-to-stinger with this creepy living nightmare!

Yet as I began to analyze the scenario, I could see how taking a sting might actually help educate the audience on the effects of the venom, and how, if it wasn't any worse than a bee sting, we could disprove the notion that all scorpion stings can be fatal.

Like I said before: You can't fully appreciate or learn anything about life if you don't face your fears. So I closed my eyes, took a deep breath, and started to plan with my crew.

Scorpions have been on this planet since prehistoric times. The type I was about to meet, the giant desert hairy scorpion, is the largest scorpion in North America, measuring around five to six inches in length. Scorpions have two body segments and

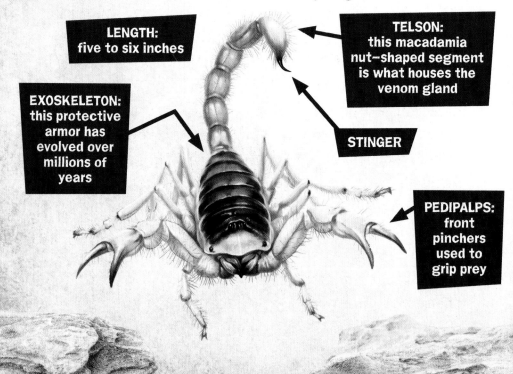

LENGTH: five to six inches

TELSON: this macadamia nut–shaped segment is what houses the venom gland

EXOSKELETON: this protective armor has evolved over millions of years

STINGER

PEDIPALPS: front pinchers used to grip prey

eight legs, making them arachnids rather than insects, which have three body segments and six legs. Only one of the almost two thousand types of scorpions in the world, the giant desert hairy is yellow with short, brown hairs covering its rigid exoskeleton. This protective armor has evolved over millions of years and is so strong that it's nearly impossible to squash the scorpion's body no matter how hard you squeeze it.

The desert hairy's massive front pedipalps, or pincers, can lock onto prey and hold on mercilessly tight, until the scorpion has a chance to flip up its tail and inflict a venomous sting. The actual stinger is located at the end of the arachnid's tail on what is referred to as the telson. This macadamia nut-shaped segment is what houses the venom gland. The needle-like tip, where the true stinger is located, is how the venom is injected into the animal's prey or used as a defense to guard it against any would-be attacker. After the prey is paralyzed by this venom, the scorpion's pincers pull apart the victim and lift it up

While thirty to forty types of scorpions can be lethal, no one has ever died from a giant hairy's sting.

to its menacing mandibles, and they further break it down into bite-size morsels. Scorpions are perfectly designed little predators, hunting insects, spiders, and sometimes even lizards, snakes, and other scorpions!

Despite the fact that the giant desert hairy scorpion looks like a nightmare from another planet, these arachnids aren't very dangerous—unless, of course, you're an insect or small vertebrate who might make a tasty lunch. While thirty to forty types of scorpions can be lethal, no one's ever died from a giant hairy's sting. In fact, it's supposed to feel no worse than a bee sting. There is one kind of scorpion in the Southwest called the bark scorpion, whose sting can inflict pain that lasts for a full six weeks, though! But the desert hairy is less fearsome, and unless you develop an allergic reaction and leave it untreated, his sting is never going to kill you.

However, that doesn't stop individuals from killing *them* all the time! Scorpions have a bad reputation, and people who find them in their houses spray them with Windex, squash them with boots, or whack them with broom bristles while sweeping them out the door. People probably don't realize that these scorpions haven't invaded their houses looking for trouble. They're just opportunists. Scorpions like to hang out in cool, dark places, and few are more appealing than the bedsheets you left in a pile next to your basement washer, or the shoes you took off at the end of the day and placed in your garage. A scorpion sees those boots and scurries inside, thinking, *This dark, stinky thing is the perfect place for a nap!*

The next morning, though, you put your shoe on, and...*Ouch!* You just got stung by a scorpion.

I was armed with a life-saving EpiPen and a brain full of research, but I was still worried as we ventured deep into the desert late that night. The Sonoran Desert is a giant playground for filming, filled with all kinds of desert animals waiting to be encountered, but we knew there was no way we could catch a scorpion during the scorching daylight hours. The giant desert hairy is

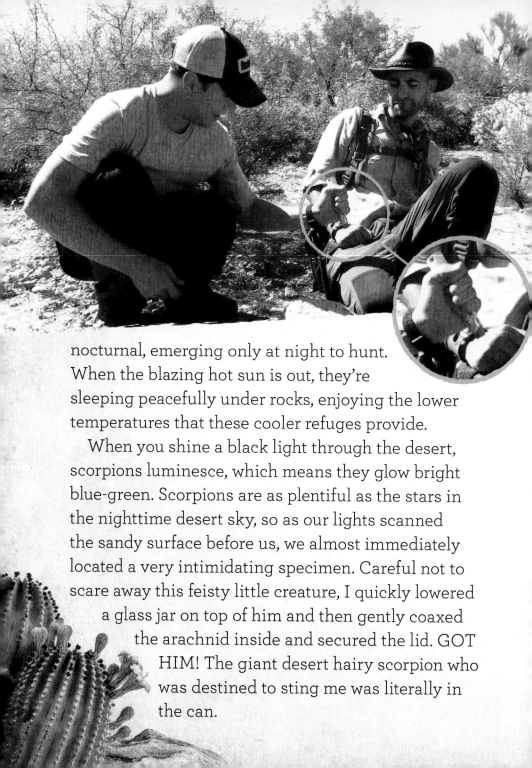

nocturnal, emerging only at night to hunt.
When the blazing hot sun is out, they're
sleeping peacefully under rocks, enjoying the lower
temperatures that these cooler refuges provide.

When you shine a black light through the desert,
scorpions luminesce, which means they glow bright
blue-green. Scorpions are as plentiful as the stars in
the nighttime desert sky, so as our lights scanned
the sandy surface before us, we almost immediately
located a very intimidating specimen. Careful not to
scare away this feisty little creature, I quickly lowered
a glass jar on top of him and then gently coaxed
the arachnid inside and secured the lid. GOT
HIM! The giant desert hairy scorpion who
was destined to sting me was literally in
the can.

Brave Wilderness was still in its infancy, but as filmmakers, we weren't so green that we thought that shooting a scene such as this one at night was a good idea. So we decided to keep this creepy-crawly overnight in a small Tupperware container with holes in the top while we slept. Then we'd hike back into the desert to film the sting scene in the morning. The scorpion wasn't entirely without his creature comforts in that cage. Even though we knew he'd be perfectly fine living in an empty space, we wanted him to be happy, so we provided him with sand and rocks to hide under. This menacing, huge-pincered, stinger-wielding being was going to get some rest that night even if Coyote Peterson didn't!

Giant desert hairy scorpions may have tiny brains, but they're smart enough to know when someone is trying to invade their space. They'll scurry away as soon as they sense a human approaching, so we had no idea how to position our little scorpion so he'd sting my hand before dashing off. Without the cameras rolling, we experimented with different ways

DID YOU KNOW?
Giant desert hairy scorpions are fluorescent, which means they glow blue-green under black light!

to get the desert hairy to sit still and sting me. I put my hand near his pincers hoping that would evoke a sting, but he refused to grab me and instead was only interested in escaping. Not once did the arachnid have an interest in grappling on, let alone inflicting a sting. Instead, he ran away, thinking, *No way! There's a hand coming at me. Time to take off!*

Part of me wishes we'd filmed these failed strikes and aired them. I think seeing a scorpion run for the hills would have helped alleviate the Coyote Pack— and the world's—misguided fear of these fascinating arachnids.

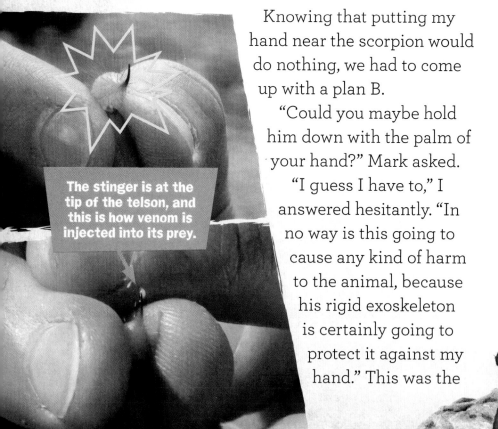

The stinger is at the tip of the telson, and this is how venom is injected into its prey.

Knowing that putting my hand near the scorpion would do nothing, we had to come up with a plan B.

"Could you maybe hold him down with the palm of your hand?" Mark asked.

"I guess I have to," I answered hesitantly. "In no way is this going to cause any kind of harm to the animal, because his rigid exoskeleton is certainly going to protect it against my hand." This was the only feasible way to provoke a sting, so we decided to go for it.

The first thing I had to do was remove the scorpion from the Tupperware container. I carefully took off the lid, tilted the plastic slightly to the side, and

Go ahead, Coyote...get your hand close and see what happens!

quickly grasped the scorpion by the back knuckle, or telson, which is the section of the tail that connects the stinger to its long tail. I knew the scorpion might swing around and extend his pedipalps up toward me in an attempt to pinch, but I wasn't going to get stung unless I let go of the telson and came into contact with the stinger.

I laid the scorpion gently on the rock in front of me, his tail still firmly grasped between my fingers.

Deep breaths, Coyote, I told myself. *This will be over before you know it.*

I hesitantly rested my hand on the arachnid's exoskeleton-armored back, pushing just a bit to

ensure he wouldn't slip out. Then I let go of the tail
and waited. The seconds seemed to draw out like
hours. Was he going to STRIKE? The scorpion's
natural defense mechanisms gradually began
to set in as it dawned upon the creature: *If this
human doesn't unpin me, I can't get away.* Then with
incredible speed, the scorpion swung his tail through
the air in an arcing motion. *Whoosh.* The stinger
struck me, and *whack!*

My fearful mind had imagined that the sensation
would be like a mousetrap slamming down on

He got
me!

the back of my
hand, but it was
far subtler. The
scorpion's stinger
is curved at the
end, and as it went
into my skin at
an angle, I could

sense its sharpness. It was like a tiny needle piercing through my epidermis—the top layer of my skin—and penetrating my hand.

"*Ahh!*" I yelped, pulling my hand up toward my face as the scorpion scurried off the rock and disappeared down into the shade. But my reaction was more from the surprise of the sting rather than any intense pain. My research had proven true: The scorpion's sting was sudden, pointed, sharp...yet much to my delight, no worse than a honey bee sting.

The reason the pain wasn't agonizing or intense is because giant desert hairy scorpion venom isn't very toxic. The scorpion is so massive relative to the insects and small animals it hunts that it can mostly immobilize its prey just with its pincers alone. Then its mandibles can rip the captured prey into bits. In short, the desert hairy doesn't rely solely on its venom to stop a meal from squirming and escaping.

"Uh, may I inquire where that scorpion

I can feel a small welt forming under my skin.

just went?" Chance asked when the camera stopped rolling.

"He's hiding in the shade on the back side of this rock," I answered, looking down. "It's dark and cool under there."

I have to be honest: I was *so* relieved that the sting of the scorpion wasn't all that bad. And I was even more relieved that I didn't have an adverse reaction, like swelling or difficulty breathing. Forget the impact of a scorpion sting; if I'd sensed an allergic reaction coming on, I would have had to jab the EpiPen into my leg!

As we hiked back to our base camp, I could feel a small welt forming under my skin. That firm, hard nodule went down after a few days.

DID YOU KNOW?

Female giant desert hairy scorpions give birth to live young and can have up to thirty-five at a time. The babies are called scorplings!

"The swelling's a bit like a spider bite," I told my crew. "It's really not bad at all."

About twelve hours after filming wrapped, I found that the sting zone was just the tiniest bit itchy, but it wasn't irritating enough for me to apply any topical cream, and I certainly did not need to seek any medical attention. I was pleased for both myself and the scorpion; a few seconds of stinging pain and some minor itching showed the Coyote Pack that giant desert hairy scorpions are nothing to be feared.

These animals should be given their space and admired from afar for the complex, fascinating—and yes, creepy-looking—creatures that they are. If Coyote Peterson being stung, which in turn was viewed by millions of people, had helped the general public realize that not all scorpions are as dangerous as advertised, then this episode had certainly done its job.

CHAPTER 3

ATTACKED BY ANTS!

HARVESTER ANT
(POGONOMYRMEX MARICOPA)

PAIN INDEX
2

Not long after our scorpion sting episode went up on YouTube, my team and I started to grasp what the audience was hungry for—more sting episodes! The Coyote Pack numbered less than a hundred thousand at that point, but they begged for me to endure more painful stings from the most fascinating, misunderstood, and most feared insects in the world. So we had no choice but to deliver!

My mom lives deep in the rugged Arizona desert, not far from where we'd filmed our scorpion episode. One day when I was visiting her, scouting out locations to encounter a new batch of desert creatures, she pulled me aside to instill a warning.

"Coyote," she said, looking concerned, "I know you're heading out on an adventure today, so I need to warn you about something."

"What's that?" I asked.

"Don't wander over there, whatever you do," she whispered, pointing to a sparse, dusty expanse behind her house. "There's a colony of harvester ants, and the other day I was stung by one. Boy, did it give me a wallop!"

Harvester ants? I wondered for a second, then shrugged it off. Nobody ever listens to their mom. *Whatever. Ants don't sound that threatening.*

Afterward, Mario and I ventured into my mom's backyard and stared into the small, shadowy burrow that housed the desert insects that had stung her. Then we then did some research and realized how wrong we were to doubt her. As the insect with the most toxic venom in the world, harvester ants would prove to be my most epic—and painful—sting to date.

The name *harvester ant* is actually a blanket term that covers hundreds of species of ants across the globe, all of whom collect seeds and store them in their nests. The little farmers of the ant world, they're sometimes also known as the agricultural ant, and they serve as entry-level pollinators when they venture out and scatter these stored seeds.

The terrifying, six-legged beasts that had launched an attack on my poor mom are the Maricopa harvester ants. Found extensively in Arizona but also present throughout the western and southwestern

United States and into Mexico, they live mostly in rural areas. Many suburban homeowners fear getting stung, so they exterminate harvester ants by pouring boiling water on their nests or baiting them with poison. But in the remote wilderness, they're abundant. In fact, this ant species is so dominant in the Arizona desert that the name *Maricopa* is usually dropped. It's simply the harvester ant, and it's notorious for the pain it can inflict!

Harvester ants are subterranean colony builders, which means that calling their homes "mounds" is a bit of a misnomer. Their colonies don't resemble tiny, sandy volcanoes, with craters on top that serve as the ants' exit door, like the homes of the common carpenter ant or the much-dreaded fire ant. Instead, they're a series of underground chambers and paths through which the ants carry seeds.

NEST ENTRANCE

DID YOU KNOW?
Harvest ants are granivores, meaning they almost exclusively feed on the seeds from plants.

They're topped with hard calcium carbonate carried from the deeper layers of the desert soil, and these cement-like roofs protect the nests from the strong winds that whip through the desert. Harvester ants also clear vegetation from the area surrounding their nests, so if you look into the desert and see patches of greenery here and there, with big, blank areas of dirt, sand, or gravel between them, chances are there are harvester ants living below. In some cases, the ants' burrows even look like crop circles, with sand pushed out from a center depression, then surrounded by concentric circles.

Unfortunately, these colonies are tough to spot unless you know what to look for, which is why someone who's hiking through the desert—especially in flip-flops or sandals—may easily step on one and get stung by an angry swarm. And when that happens...*Ouch!*

Most people may not realize that, while all ant species can bite, not all of them sting. Like fire ants, harvester ants have stingers on the base of their abdomens, and they're not afraid to use them. When they do, they unleash the most toxic venom of any insect in the world! That's right; it's twenty times more toxic than a honey bee's sting. But the venom yield ratio is very low. What that means is that if a harvester ant stings you, it's going to hurt like crazy because it packs such a punch, but not much venom actually *goes into* your body. A honey bee's sting injects more venom into you, but the aftereffects are less painful. There are no reported cases of anyone dying from harvester ant stings. However, if you were stung hundreds of times and suffered a severe allergic reaction, death could be possible. So this is not an insect you ever want to tangle with.

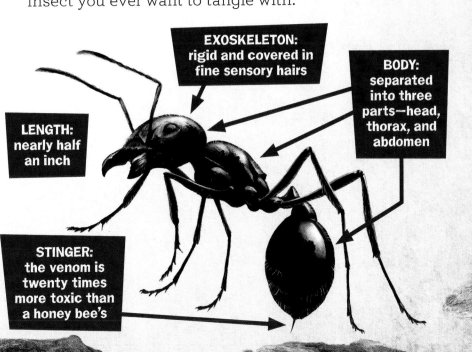

EXOSKELETON: rigid and covered in fine sensory hairs

BODY: separated into three parts—head, thorax, and abdomen

LENGTH: nearly half an inch

STINGER: the venom is twenty times more toxic than a honey bee's

These "jaws" are used to grab any attacker of the colony before the ant lowers its abdomen and fiercely stings with its needle–sharp stinger.

The venom contains a pheromone that, when released in a sting, sets off an alarm that attracts other ants.

These tiny desert insects have no other defense mechanism to ward off predators, so they're incredibly fearless and they'll be aggressive when necessary. You'd never know they were so vicious at first glance, though. When Mario and I ventured outside and carefully stepped around the nest, we watched from a safe distance as a few emerged from the ground. They were sizeable—nearly half an inch long—with strong, sturdy bodies that were separated, like all ants, into three parts. They were dark brown (though they can also be mustard yellow in color), and they had fine hairs all over their bodies and their six long legs. What struck me most, though, was how cute they all were.

"Look at them, Mario!" I said excitedly. "They're carrying little leaves and plants in their mandibles, just like you'd see in one of those ant farms you had as a kid!"

Don't be fooled, though. Right at the base of their heads are intimidating, chomping mandibles. These "jaws" are used to grab any attacker of the colony before the ant lowers its abdomen and fiercely stings with its needle-sharp stinger.

The incredibly toxic venom packed inside the harvester ant's stinger is not your usual toxin, either. Yes, it's some of the most poisonous in the world, but it also contains a pheromone that, when released in a sting, sets off an alarm that attracts other ants. It's as if the ants can smell an invasion, and they come running, ready to fight. This rallying call is especially useful against the hungry desert predators who aim to eat harvester ants, like horned lizards, who will attack and decimate an entire colony in a matter of hours.

Unfortunately, I didn't think about a multi-ant attack being a possibility before I encountered the harvester ant. That's right; the Brave Wilderness

I didn't think about a multi-ant attack being a possibility before I encountered the harvester ant.

crew—especially me—was woefully underprepared for the chaos that ensued when I placed my hands on top of this colony of startled, angry harvester ants who were poised for attack.

Early morning in my mom's backyard is a perfect location for filming, so the day after Mario and I inspected the harvester ant colony, we carried our gear outside to film.

"It doesn't look like there are that many ants in that nest," I said to Mark and Mario when I laid my eyes on a handful of innocent-looking ants running around on the surface. "So why don't I just stick my hands right on top of it?"

"Sounds great," Mark replied. "The ones that are visible will climb onto you. You'll get a couple of stings, and we'll record the effects."

Mark, Mario, and I had decided that, to really challenge myself and excite the viewers, I'd set a time limit for how long I'd rest my hands on top of the harvester ant colony. At first, I estimated a short span of fifteen seconds.

"Let's do thirty seconds!" Mark shouted.

"Thirty seconds—that sounds like a challenge," I answered. "But let's make it a nice, round number. I can do sixty."

Mario just shook his head. His research had told him this was going to be *very* painful.

I tucked my pants inside my boots to prevent ants from crawling inside and rolled up my sleeves to give them a target for stinging. I set up a GoPro camera in front of the ant's burrow, which I was super excited about because I knew I'd get great close-up shots of the ants crawling. Then I looked around, taking note of my surroundings, and nodded to Mark and Mario.

Time for an ant attack!

Time for an ant attack!

I crouched down, extended my fingers as wide as I could, and placed my hands lightly on the ground, right above the

undisturbed sandy area that was the opening to the ant's colony. *Thump.* I tapped my palms lightly on the ground, signaling to the ants that their underground catacomb of intricacies had been invaded. I waited for a split second, and they answered the call. *Something's trying to eat us! Attack!*

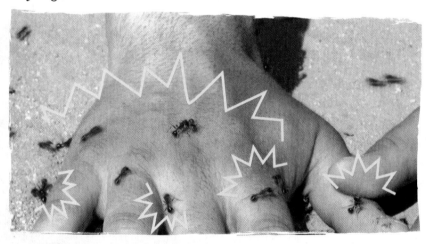

Almost immediately, ants began spilling out in every direction from the doorway of the colony. *Oh my gosh, there are a lot more ants in there than I thought there would be!* I said to myself as ants began swarming up my fingers, onto my hands, and up my forearms. Within seconds, one stung me.

"*Ack!*" I screamed, my body jolting backward just a bit.

Then came another horrendous, fiery sting.
Then another, then another, then another.

I couldn't wrap my brain around how fast the ants
seemed to appear out of nowhere as they aggressively
swarmed me. These harvester ants were in full-on
attack mode, running up my hands and along my arms.
After about thirty seconds passed, some managed
to get under my shirtsleeves and onto my chest. By
forty-five seconds, a few had cleverly worked their way
into my pants, fanning across my legs. Still, I kept my
hands suspended within attacking grasp of the colony,
and I watched in horror as more and more piled on.

Then an ant crawled onto my neck, bit down, and
inflicted a searing wallop of a sting. That's when
I really lost it. The thought of waiting a few more

seconds before he scurried onto my face or toward my eyes was just too much. Mom was right. These ants were fearless, and they wanted nothing more than to take the invader, in this case Coyote Peterson, down and out!

Like I said, a harvester ant's attack is two-fold: He bites down with his mandibles on an attacker's body, then quickly thrusts his stinger deep into it. The bite has almost no feeling to it; it's more like a slight pinch. It's the release of the alkaloid venom into your body that produces a sharp, burning sensation. The ant can then sting again and again, and he will do so until the venom in its body runs out.

The site of the stings burned so badly that, when sixty seconds was finally up, I felt as if my life had been spared. I immediately stood up and began shaking my arms and legs to clear the remaining ants from my body. I ripped off my shirt, as the ants inside were continuing their onslaught with incredible aggression. Almost immediately, reddish-purple welts started to form at the site of the stings. They felt as if

they were on fire, and that burning extended out from the sting onto the surrounding skin. In fact, I could see that my arms had started to swell up, the pain radiating in waves all over my exhausted, traumatized body.

I was also light-headed and dizzy, and I worried that at any moment I might pass out. Mark and Mario could clearly see that I had taken more stings than originally anticipated, and they quickly wrangled me in so I could deliver an outro for the episode.

"I think, half an hour from now if I'm okay, there's a good chance that in the future, I'm going to be able to get up close, and possibly stung, by the bullet ant. I'm Coyote Peterson, Be Brave, Stay Wild...we'll see ya on the next adventure!"

I shuffled back to my mom's house, swatting at my arms, legs, and neck, convinced that the ants were still swarming me. Then I peeled off the rest of my clothes, stepped in the shower, and turned the water all the way to cold. As I let the ice-cold water pour over me, I started to count my stings.

Oh man! I gasped. *There are probably fifty or sixty stings on me! There are even some behind my ears!*

These stings weren't like your ordinary mosquito bites, either. They were isolated reddish-purple welts

that were nearly the size of dimes and spread out all over my body. I knew that my white blood cells were flooding the area of the stings, dispersing the venom, but it wasn't happening fast enough for me. After stepping out of the shower, I still felt out of it. Even when I walked back outside to meet up with Mario and Mark half an hour later, I wasn't doing much better.

"What just happened to me?" I asked them. "I feel like I got blasted by a fireball."

"That was pretty crazy," Mark replied. "But I have no doubt that it's going to turn into an amazing episode—despite the fact that it was complete chaos. But I bet the GoPro shots are going to turn out pretty cool!"

Sure enough, when we went into postproduction days later and looked at the footage, it was clear we had enough incredible content, despite the chaos, to make a wild yet educational episode. I still had welts on my arms, a bit of tenderness in places, and periods of itching now and then, but I knew I'd filmed something the Coyote Pack would love. In the GoPro shots, the ants marched in front of the lens, simulating the effect of them swarming my arm. The lighting was fantastic, and even in the midst of my agony, I talked enough about the ants to allow our viewers to

DID YOU KNOW?

A nest's lifespan is reliant on the lifespan of its queen, which is about 17–25 years.

learn something about these marvelous, fearless little beasts. So we cut the footage, edited and re-edited, added some cool music, put a small "ant timer" in the lower left-hand corner of the screen, and *bam!* We had an episode.

Boy, did it take off! "Ant Attack!" was our fastest video to one hundred thousand views. We'd officially gone viral in our own little animal adventure pocket of YouTube!

Best of all, the comments I received from the Coyote Pack turned me on to the man who'd change the course of my adventures in the world of insect stings. Thanks to the audience, I was about to follow the path of the one and only architect of the world-renowned insect sting pain index: entomologist Justin Schmidt!

CHAPTER 4

BURNING RING OF FIRE!

FIRE ANTS
(SOLENOPSIS INVICTA)

PAIN INDEX
2

Before I ever got stung by a merciless wasp called the tarantula hawk, or watched with horror as a velvet ant injected her toxic venom into my blood, or plunged my shaking hands into a mound of swarming fire ants, Justin Schmidt had done it all. A world-renowned entomologist who works at the University of Arizona's Center for Insect Science, Schmidt published a book in 2016 called *The Sting of the Wild: The Story of the Man Who Got Stung for Science.*

In it, he recounts getting stung by over eighty separate types of ants, wasps, and bees, and he ranks the intensity and pain of their stings on a scale of one to four, with one being the weakest and four being the most powerful. This simple yet brilliant system is now called the Schmidt insect sting pain index, and when I got turned on to it, it became my trusted road map on all my insect escapades.

The harvester ant episode aired in January 2016, and Justin published and began promoting his book just a couple of months later, in March. I suspect some of the Coyote Pack heard his interview on NPR or read about his book in *Discover* magazine, because a few of them soon mentioned him in the comments section of the harvester ant posting. *Who is this guy?* I wondered. *He sounds like the true King of Sting!*

I bought Justin's book right away and dove in. I loved it, and it caused a million questions and ideas to spring into my head. *Who knew there were so many stinging insects in the world?* I thought. Justin described them beautifully, illustrating the pain from their stings in eloquent yet never overly scientific language. I realized immediately that his research paved the way for me to embark on my next wild foray into the world of insects, and his sting pain index raised the stakes for both me and my viewers. After all, if Justin Schmidt ranked the pain from the warrior wasp as a four, with the duration of pain lasting 150 minutes, I was going to have to experience that for myself! The Coyote Pack demanded it, and they deserved it.

Like I always say, though, you have to learn to walk before you can

The pain from the warrior wasp sting can last 150 minutes.

run. I needed to work up to the velvet ant (a three) and the bullet ant (a four). Besides, while seeing me getting stung by fierce insects like the tarantula hawk might feel exotic and thrilling, these creatures aren't necessarily relatable. Most of my viewers don't ever find themselves in the middle of the Sonoran Desert or deep in the dense rain forests of Costa Rica. If I wanted Brave Wilderness to be a truly educational yet exhilarating experience for fans, shouldn't I explore insects you might find in your own backyard? Shouldn't I uncover the biological ambushes that threaten to ruin your picnic or, worse, send you to your local hospital in anaphylactic shock? Absolutely!

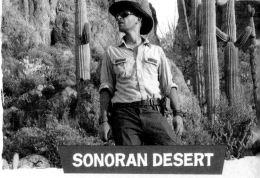

SONORAN DESERT

COSTA RICA

That's why I chose to come face-to-face with the insect I would never—not even for a million dollars—allow myself to get stung by again: the red imported fire ant!

Fire ants are an ever-present menace in the lower half of the United States, including the Southwest,

California, Texas, the Southeast, Florida, and even into mid-Atlantic states like Maryland. There are actually over two hundred species of fire ants in the world, but only a handful exist in the US. Several of those species are native to this country, but others are invasive, like the red imported fire ant. Rumored to have the most painful sting of all American fire ants, this much-detested foreign invader made its way from South America to Mobile, Alabama, in the 1930s, on a ship containing soil. Because of the damage ants now cause to crops and wildlife, the US government spends millions of dollars a year fighting them!

Fire ants are significantly smaller than harvester ants, at about an eighth to a quarter of an inch. With their three parts (the head, thorax, and abdomen), six spindly legs, chomping mandibles, and sizable stinger situated at the end of their abdomens, they resemble harvester ants if you look at them closely. But unlike harvester ants, they're not uniform in color; the first

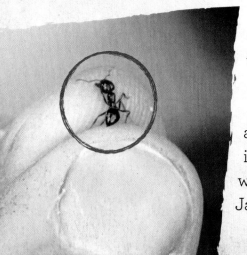

two sections of their bodies are copper-colored, while their abdomen is dark brown, almost black.

We don't have any fire ants in Ohio, let alone red imported fire ants, so before we filmed our episode in January 2016, I'd never seen

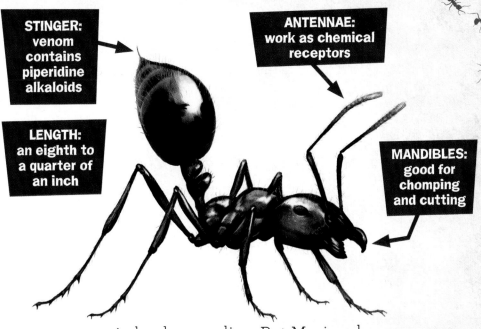

STINGER: venom contains piperidine alkaloids

ANTENNAE: work as chemical receptors

LENGTH: an eighth to a quarter of an inch

MANDIBLES: good for chomping and cutting

one except in books or online. But Mario, who grew up in South Florida, was well familiar with them.

"Man, we've got them everywhere at home," he said. "I'm warning you; I've gotten stung by them before, and it's bad. Like, really, really bad."

Maybe I was feeling like a tough guy after my encounter with the harvester ants, but I brushed him off. *No way*, I remember thinking, *they can't be half as painful as the harvester ant. Besides, Justin Schmidt ranked them as only a two on the insect sting pain index, with the pain lasting five minutes. That's nothing!*

Mario seemed lost in some terrible childhood memory,

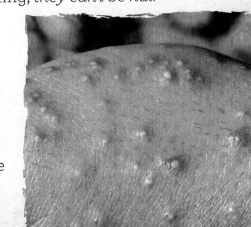

and he kept talking. "After you get stung—and trust me, you'll get stung everywhere—these itchy white pustules form on your skin. They're an unsightly nightmare that you want nothing to do with."

But I still didn't take him seriously. "Mario," I replied, "I have a very high pain tolerance, and I didn't have a bad reaction to the harvester ant. I bet I'll only have some swelling...no pustules."

Right? If I'd faced the harvester ant and come out in one piece, I could face anything.

We knew that finding a hearty fire ant mound would be a piece of cake, so we searched for a location close to amenities so we wouldn't have to spend our time driving or hiking into the middle of nowhere rather than filming. Mario suggested Homestead, Florida, a small town southwest of Miami, on the edge of Everglades National Park. When we got there, we immediately found a few anthills.

DID YOU KNOW?
Ant colonies can have as many as 250,000 workers!

Any native of Texas, Florida, or the Southeast has a story about throwing a picnic blanket on the ground, sitting down on it to enjoy a nice afternoon with friends and a cold glass of iced tea, and then feeling licks of fire curling up their legs. *Owww!* As they jump up, kick off their shoes, and frantically brush at their ankles, they realize what transpired:

Mounds may be only slightly raised or as tall as eighteen inches, and they don't have craterous openings on top like harvester ant nests do.

FIRE ANT MOUND

They just happened upon a fire ant mound, one of America's most notorious biological land mines! These large, elevated, mountain-shaped areas are often camouflaged against their surroundings because they're constructed from the same materials. Ants build with soil, gravel, clay, sand, or whatever they can find close-by. Mounds may be only slightly raised or as tall as eighteen inches, and they don't have craterous openings on top like carpenter ant nests do. Similar to harvester ants, fire ants enter their nests through underground tunnels, which can extend down into the earth as far as ten feet.

What you likely won't see on a mound, however, are the ants themselves. These tiny creatures are busy inside, carrying plants, laying eggs, or digging more tunnels. But when that nest is disturbed, the ornery inhabitants go on high alert and attack with full force.

"Are you sure you want to go through with this?" Mario kept asking as we approached our chosen fire ant mound.

"Well, no," I finally admitted, realizing all his talk about burning pain and white pustules had gotten to me. "But I really don't think this is going to hurt that badly. The ant is so much smaller than the harvester ant, so I can't see how the pain's going to be that awful."

Little did I realize that fire ant pain doesn't just come from the intensity of a sting, but from the sheer *number* of stings. And, boy, was I about to be stung *a lot*!

Part of my confusion may have resulted from misunderstanding Justin Schmidt's insect sting pain index. When Justin ranked the red fire ant as a two, he was only speaking to his experience, which involved just a handful of isolated stings. But few people who stumble upon a mound are ever stung by just two or three fire ants. In an actual fire ant attack, these insects quickly become agressive, form a furious swarm, and then sting en masse.

A timer had worked well for us in the harvester ant episode, so we decided to use it again. Even though

DID YOU KNOW?
Fire ants are highly aggressive, and swarm anything that disturbs the nest. Once a fire ant contacts its target, it will sting multiple times until forcibly removed.

Mario was doubtful, I estimated that I could stick my Coyote paws into the mound and hold them there for sixty seconds. Or, at least, I'd try as hard as possible to make that happen.

"All right. If you guys are ready, let's go for this," I said to Mark and Mario just before we began filming. And then, *lights, camera, action*, we were rolling.

My heart was pounding, and beads of sweat formed on my brow as I paced back and forth, holding a camera in my hand. I understood the task that lay before me, but I was starting to get really scared. *What if Mario is right? What if I do get pustules? Or, worse, what if I go into anaphylactic shock and have to be hospitalized?* I pushed those thoughts aside, adjusted my hat, crouched down, and delivered my iconic intro. "I'm Coyote Peterson and I'm about to enter the Sting Zone with the fire ants. You guys ready? One...two...

Fire ant pain doesn't just come from the intensity of a sting, but from the sheer number of stings.

three!" I placed my GoPro in the crumbling soil so we'd have close-up footage of the swarming little pests. Then I thrust my hands deep in the mound. The ring of fire had been ignited!

"Ow, ow, ow!" The first stings came fast and furious within seconds. "Holy cow, that's a lot of stings!" I

screamed, shocked more by the rapid-fire blast of the ants' attack than I was by the pain. Then scorching, roasting agony set in. My hands were hot, as if I'd plunged them right into a pile of campfire embers, and that heat was all I could feel. There was no sharpness— no repeating, isolated pricks—just an absolute, extreme sensation of being on fire.

Unlike the harvester ants, the fire ants didn't want to race up my arms and into my clothes; they were content to run around on my hands and forearms, stinging me repeatedly.

"This is definitely worse than the harvester ants!" I screamed about thirty seconds in. And it most certainly was. These fire ants had hooked their tiny mandibles into my arms and held on. But it wasn't the bites that hurt. In fact, they didn't even break my skin. It was the alkaloid venom—called isosolenopsin—that burned as it went into my bloodstream. These stings were faster, more immediate, and more in unison than the harvester ant—and there were a heck of a lot more of them. I estimate that there were hundreds of thousands of fire ants living in that mound, and what looked like hundreds were on my hands and arms, stinging me again and again.

"I can't do it! I've gotta stop!" I screamed after forty seconds. I stood up, clenched my hands into fists to stop the blood flow, and, for a split second, considered sticking

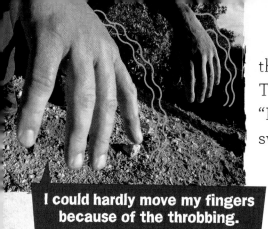

I could hardly move my fingers because of the throbbing.

them back into the mound. Then I realized I was crazy. "I think my hands are swelling right now," I said to Mark. And, in fact, they were. I could see my veins bulging against my tight, stretched skin.

About fifteen minutes after my plunge into the ring of fire, my hands were still burning. The intensity had lessened, but it sure hadn't gone away. I'd just become accustomed to the uncomfortable, low-level smoldering. My hands were fully swollen, and I could see shiny white pustules—which itched like crazy—forming at the sites of the stings.

I didn't touch my wounds, though. Instead, we stopped filming, and I fished out a water bottle containing a yellow liquid from my backpack. As

I counted about three hundred pustules on the fronts and backs of my hands and up my arms.

Mark and Mario cringed, they turned the cameras back on. Then I poured my own urine over the pustules, and warmth washed over me. The relief was immediate. *Ahhh.* In one of the most basic chemical reactions in the world, the ammonia in my urine

neutralized the alkaloid in the venom, and my hands cooled down.

But that relief was short-term. When I went to bed that night, my hands were so hot that I wrapped them in cold, wet washcloths to keep down the temperature. I slept fitfully, tossing and turning, and when I woke up the next morning, I rolled over on my pillow, put my hands to my face, and was shocked at how hot they still were.

Then I got up and stared down at my sore hands. Oh my gosh! They looked like gigantic red meat mitts! I was a hideous beast, like someone who had contracted a weird, ancient disease that was eating my flesh away. I counted about three hundred pustules on the fronts and backs of my hands and up my arms, and I could hardly move my fingers because of the throbbing.

"We're not taking you to get breakfast today unless you put some gloves on your hands," Mark and Mario said, laughing, when I met them in the hotel lobby.

Except they weren't joking. So I stuck my hands in my pockets and kept them there till my food arrived. Then I sheepishly lifted my fork to my lips, slouching over so no one could see how hideous I was.

Those pustules stayed on my hands for at least a solid month. They weren't just white, swollen, and unsightly—they also itched like crazy. I bought a pair of batting gloves that I'd wear out, but the problem was that I had to take them off to scratch. Sometimes I'd scratch so hard that I'd break open the pustules, and—much like poison ivy blisters—pus would ooze out. Then a divot would appear in my flesh.

Sometimes people would notice my gloves and look at me as if I were nuts.

"What happened to your hands?" they'd ask.

"Let me tell you the story," I'd reply, laughing. "I intentionally put my hands into a mound of fire ants!"

Months later, my skin finally began to heal, but a canvas of scars remained as a constant reminder of that day. Two and a half years later, those scars have finally faded, but I'll never forget what I went through. Without a doubt, the fire ant encounter made for the most mentally taxing month of my life.

The good news was that the episode went viral almost immediately. It racked up a hundred thousand views in its first hour, and at this point in time, it

boasts a whopping sixteen million views. I'd attribute much of that success to the fact that people are familiar with fire ants, and sometimes the things that are closest to you are the scariest. Think of fire ants as the monsters hiding in your closet: You don't ever want to face them, so you're always more than happy to have someone else do it for you. In this scenario, that is exactly what I did...and who I became.

I'd never endure a fire ant attack again, knowing what I know now. I couldn't bear another month of feeling like an outcast, my gloved hands tucked inside my pockets so people wouldn't run away from me in terror. But I am grateful that the episode put Brave Wilderness firmly on the map *and* taught viewers about the dangerous biological land mine known as the fire ant.

Unfortunately for me, though, there were many more land mines to come!

CHAPTER 5

EUROPEAN PAPER WASP (POLISTES DOMINULA)

THE BUZZ OF BACKYARD BUGS!

Allow me to jump into my time machine and zip ahead...long after the fire ants, past the time of the velvet ant, and even beyond the exotic, foreign realm of the bullet ant, which I know you're all dying to read about. Imagine us landing squarely in an ordinary backyard just outside of my hometown in Columbus, Ohio, where I'll introduce you to yet another common biological land mine: the European paper wasp!

Why should you care about such a run-of-the-mill insect, who's not half as strange and alien as the tarantula hawk, or as ferocious as the warrior wasp, with a sting that Justin Schmidt describes as "like being chained in the flow of an active volcano"? (Ouch!) You should pay attention because these are bugs most, if not all, of you are going to encounter at some point in your lives. When you do, your impulse may be to scream and run in the opposite direction. That or perhaps you might be foolish enough to try to knock down their nests with a broom, which will cause them to swarm and most certainly sting you. Or, if you're eight-year-old Coyote Peterson, you'll

dress yourself in three layers of clothing, two baseball gloves, a scarf, and a winter ski mask topped off with swimming googles, then join your friends as you try to get dangerously close in an attempt to admire their nest and catch one in a glass jar. (Yes, this happened, and, believe it or not, I escaped without being stung.)

Trust me, though, you shouldn't do any of these things, and not just to save your own skin. You should respect wasps because these insects are very important to the ecosystem. The paper wasp—like millions of other stinging insects around the world—is a fascinating, helpful creature who deserves care and a shot at life. When I was intentionally stung by a paper wasp in 2017, it was my goal to show the Coyote Pack just how cool these flying creatures truly are and also how to treat a sting, if you were ever unfortunate enough to take one.

In my little corner of Ohio, there are all kinds of stinging bees, wasps, and hornets, including the dramatic, gorgeous blue-winged wasp, the cicada killer—a wasp that, you guessed it, likes to hunt down cicadas in the summer—and the sweat bee, a hardworking pollinator who can be quite aggressive, especially if you're sweaty. When I headed out to film the "Stung By a Yellow Jacket" episode, I knew I'd end the day getting stung by something—but at the time of production I wasn't sure what. I suspected, however, that I'd encounter the bug that most Ohioans think of as a nuisance and an enemy: the European paper wasp.

Paper wasps are often called yellow jackets, but they're technically not the same species of wasp. That differentiation has been lost in conversation, though, and these days most people simply refer to paper wasps under the blanket term *yellow jackets*. That's what I did in the video. But for clarity's sake, in this chapter I'll call this insect the paper wasp.

LENGTH:
half an inch
to three-
quarters of
an inch

WINGS:
provide aerial
speed and
agility

STINGER:
capable of
repetitive
stings

COLOR:
pattern is
aposematic
coloration

There are two hundred species of paper wasps in the world, with twenty-two of those living in the US and eight living in Ohio. One of those species, of

PAPER WASP

course, is the European paper wasp: a slender, half-inch to three-quarter-inch insect whose yellow and black stripes extend along the length of the three parts of its body. That bright color pattern is referred to as aposematic coloration, which is a way for creatures to warn anything that threatens them to stay away. Like the eyelash viper, lionfish, or poison frog, their colors signal, *Hey! You can't miss me! I'm either poisonous or venomous! I'll sting, bite, slime, or spike you! You have been warned....Now stay away!*

YELLOW JACKET

The reason many people—including me—group paper wasps with yellow jackets is because they look so much alike. However, there are some definite differences. First, paper wasps are longer and leaner than yellow jackets, who tend to appear a bit plump. Paper wasps' bodies and wings are more black than yellow; yellow jackets' dominant color is yellow, hence the name. Paper

wasps also fly with their legs sharply pointing down, while yellow jackets don't.

The easiest way to tell the two species apart, however, is by the placement of their nests. Paper wasps build their hives on the outdoor rafters or eaves of people's homes, on the outside of mailboxes or light posts, or up in trees. I'm sure you've heard stories about someone going to get the mail and coming back swollen up with stings. That person likely reached into the mailbox without seeing a hive tucked secretly away on the wooden post, slammed the box shut, and was swarmed by paper wasps. A lot of people worry that wasp nests up in rafters or perched high on your porch might fall, but they won't. The nests are secured tightly with stems the wasps have built, wrapping them around the supporting structure. Yellow jackets, on the other hand, build their homes on the ground or in holes in trees, so the real risk to you is stepping on them. Or, if you were me a few summers

DID YOU KNOW?

Not all yellow-and-black wasps are yellow jackets! There are actually over 300 species and subspecies in the genus *Polistes*, and many of them have yellow-and-black markings.

CELL

WASP EGGS

DID YOU KNOW?
A mature colony may have
over 36 members and can build
nests with over 100 cells.

ago, accidentally mowing over them. Boy, was that a big, painful surprise!

Both types of wasps build similarly intricate nests, though. They do so by chewing wood or plants with their mandibles, forming them into a mash with the help of their saliva. This mash hardens and becomes a sort of filmy papier-mâché that's light brown in color. But while yellow jacket nests are spherical and closed, paper wasp nests may be slightly oblong and contain round, often-empty holes. If you find one and see what looks like cotton stuck inside one of those holes, that's actually the wasps' eggs and larvae.

Paper wasps are some of nature's most effective gardeners, which is another reason why I believe it's just plain wrong to disturb or kill them. While yellow jackets primarily eat nectar, fruit, other insects, and sweet, sticky human food—like the Dairy Queen Blizzard that Mark, Mario, and I tried to lure them with

DID YOU KNOW?
Paper wasp nests are
abandoned every fall. Most
overwintering females
will build a new nest every
spring, instead of adopting
an old one.

during the episode—paper wasps also subsist on other insects and their eggs. In fact, they'll almost completely clear your gardens of pest larvae if you give them the chance. And when they do prey on actual insects (rather than their eggs), they sting them, paralyze them, and carry them back to their own nests. Then they store them, alive but immobile, next to their eggs. When those eggs hatch, the larvae eat them! Crazy and gross, but fascinating, huh?

Keeping a paralyzed bug hostage—then feeding its living body to your baby—may sound savage. But paper wasps are far from aggressive. In fact, while yellow jackets may come at you just because you're walking near their hives, paper wasps will typically only sting if you violate and attempt to destroy their nests and kill their young. That's why, when I finally caught a paper wasp in the contraption I dubbed the Bug Sucker

BUG SUCKER 5000

5000, I pretty much had to force the wasp to sting me. At the end of the day—and even though their stings pack a punch—paper wasps are generally gentle insects.

When Mark, Mario, and I headed out into a public park in Westerville, Ohio, I didn't anticipate that whichever backyard bug I'd lure into stinging me would cause me much pain. That wasn't the purpose of filming that day, after all. I'd been stung by wasps before—like my unfortunate mowing incident—and I knew that the discomfort would be sudden and sharp, and leave my skin swollen and hot to the touch. But as Justin Schmidt described in *The Sting of the Wild*, the pain would only last five to ten minutes before some low-level itching set in. That's why he listed the paper wasp as only a two on his sting pain index.

I also felt prepared because I'd partnered with a company called Sting-Kill, and they'd armed me with a set of benzocaine-and-menthol swabs that would ease the pain and itching when I rubbed them on my skin. I'd used Sting-Kill before, and it worked like a charm. It gave me about as much relief as pouring my own urine on my fire ant stings did, in fact, but

without the stink, and without grossing out myself, my crew, and the entire Coyote Pack!

Whether I could actually catch a backyard bug that day, though, was anybody's guess.

A few days before, I'd ordered a cute little toy online called the Extreme Bug Vac. The suction was anything *but* extreme, though, so I decided to take it apart and make my own bug sucker. Inside the toy was a small containment chamber made of hard plastic, with a magnifying glass on top and mesh on the bottom that would ensure a trapped bug could still breathe. I took the chamber out of the vacuum and set it aside. Then I took a Dirt Devil with a tube attachment, cut the tube, and taped the containment capsule to the tube using black electrical tape. We renamed my crazy device the Bug Sucker 5000, tested it to out to make sure it could actually suck and trap an insect (it could!), and, voilà! We were on our way to catching some bugs—or at least we hoped.

Because I wasn't really sure I could find a stinging bug in that Westerville public park, much less catch one, I'd called a few of my friends that morning and left them voice mails.

"Hey, do me a favor," I'd said. "Can you go outside

your houses and see if you have any wasp nests, maybe up under the eaves or near the gutter? I'm filming an episode about wasps today."

No one called me back. Why would they? Most people are afraid of paper wasps or think their nests are unsightly, so they'll remove them immediately.

But after a few hours of wandering around the park, finding next to nothing, we got a call from my friend Jasper Applewood.

"Coyote," he said, "I have a very small wasp nest right on my back porch. I was going to spray with insecticide, but it's so small I figured, *Why bother? There are only a couple of wasps in there.*"

It was perfect!

"Don't do anything," I said. "I'll be there soon."

With my Bug Sucker 5000 resting safely on the seat next to me, I drove as fast as I could to Jasper's house and headed into his big, grassy backyard. Looking up toward the eaves at the top of his porch roof, I spied the paper wasp nest immediately. Success! Small, light brown, and filmy, with several open holes full of larvae—it was just what I hoped for. Best of all, there were three paper wasps sitting right on the surface, and their wings were propped out, as if they'd spied me, too.

I grabbed a step stool Jasper had left on the porch, pulled the Bug Sucker 5000 out of my backpack, and attached a GoPro to the vacuum tube so I could get some cool close-up shots. Mario and Mark positioned themselves next to me—Mark holding the entomology net as a backup, as well as a camera—and we hoped for the best.

The wasps haven't flown off yet, I thought, *so let's see how this goes.*

One giant sucking sound rang out across the porch, and two of the wasps immediately flew away. Darn! But as I moved the Bug Sucker just a bit closer to the hive, I caught one! "Yes, yes, yes!" I screamed.

Mark came a little closer with the bug net and raised it just in case one of the escaped wasps flew by. Suddenly, we watched as one swooped in from the left, his beady eyes clearly on that paper wasp home turf. *Vroom!* I turned the Bug Sucker back on, and sure

It's getting away!

Yes, yes, yes!

enough, I captured specimen number two! *Great success!* Two safely contained stinging wasps is an ideal situation for us to film a classic insect sting episode. If one flies away during filming, or if I drop it from the entomology forceps, I have another as backup.

At this point in my foray into the world of stings, the Brave Wilderness crew and I had perfected our filming setup. We had a controlled environment close by with a small table, my Sting-Kill, the forceps, and an EpiPen in the unlikely event of an allergic reaction. We headed to our secure film set, and I took a deep breath, ready to enter the Sting Zone.

Whew, I thought, breathing out. *This never gets easier.*

With the cameras rolling, I removed the capsule from the Bug Sucker and carefully placed one wasp into the entomology net. Even though I knew paper wasps have a hard exoskeleton, I didn't want to crush this particular insect—and I definitely didn't want

to rip or damage his two long, delicate wings. I then carefully grasped the wasp with the forceps and placed him on my forearm.

One, two, three seconds passed. I shifted the bug just a bit, and he stung.

"Ah!" I said, pulling the wasp and the forceps away from my arm. My reaction looked dramatic, but the sting wasn't that bad at all. It was just as I remembered: sharp and sudden like a giant pinprick, but not excruciating. Exactly as Justin Schmidt described in his book.

Over the course of the next thirty seconds, the wasp stung me three more times. He tried to fly away, but he landed on the table and I grabbed him with the forceps and returned him to my arm. He was clearly upset: *What is this human doing? Doesn't he realize he's being stung?* The wasp stung me one more time for good measure, his stinger lodging itself in my arm while the abdomen pumped it up and down, releasing its mildly potent venom. Like ants, wasps can sting repeatedly.

Several raised white welts had formed.

But unlike bees, their stingers don't contain barbs, so they don't detach when the insect stings. In fact, bees will let their venom sacs rip out of their abdomens after a sting, allowing them to escape while the sac keeps pumping venom into their victim. Unfortunately, this means the bee may die, though—contrary to popular belief—death doesn't always occur.

This paper wasp definitely didn't die. Instead, when I returned him to his capsule, he jumped in happily, joining his hivemate. I then applied the Sting-Kill to my arm, where a silver dollar-size red area, with several

raised white welts, had formed. The relief was immediate. The benzocaine numbed the site of the sting, and the menthol cooled it, masking the pain and itching.

RELOCATED HOME

The discomfort lasted only about ten minutes, though I did feel a bit of itching and light-headedness through the afternoon. Soon after we filmed the wrap up and outro, I relocated the wasps' nest from Jasper's house to a nearby tree. My hope was that they would recommit to their nest and continue on with their happy lives away from human activity. Watching these two beautiful, misunderstood insects return to their homes, I knew this episode would educate the Coyote Pack, and in the process save a few wasps. And that, most certainly, was a good thing for everyone.

CHAPTER 6

THE NEXT LEVEL of PAIN!

VELVET ANT
(DASYMUTILLA OCCIDENTALIS)

PAIN INDEX
3

By the beginning of August 2016, I'd overcome my fears about the giant desert hairy scorpion, an arachnid whose massive, curved stinger and lobster-like pedipalps haunted me as a child. I'd conquered the harvester ant, an unexpectedly brutal insect whose vicious sting left reddish-purple welts all over my body. And I'd challenged myself against the fire ant, a biological land mine who left unsightly white pustules all over my swollen hands and arms, scarring me for months. These insect encounters sound horrific—and much of the time, they were—but I faced them for the education and enjoyment of the Coyote Pack. The Brave Wilderness crew and I also had our marching orders; we'd started to climb Justin Schmidt's insect sting pain index, and we couldn't abandon it without experiencing where the challenge ended. That, of course, was the bullet ant—whose sting Schmidt described as the most painful in the world.

But everyone knows that a fireworks display needs a few big explosions before the grand finale. We couldn't face the bullet ant without a few more dramatic encounters that would tease and tantalize our viewers. Our next stop was none other than an insect with a terrifying, half-inch stinger (yes, you read that right!). Meet the velvet ant, also known as the cow killer!

Velvet ants are actually a species of wasp.

Truth be told, velvet ants aren't ants at all; they're actually a species of wasp, though their appearance would lead you to believe otherwise. The females don't have wings, so they crawl along the ground on their legs, just like ants do. The males do have wings, but since they're often flying around, looking for plants to pollinate, they're typically hard to spot. Most people only ever see wingless females, and that's why the confusion with ants has stuck.

There are actually around eight thousand species of velvet ants in the world, but the one I planned to get stung by was the red velvet ant, also known as the eastern velvet ant. This alias is another misnomer since red velvet ants can be found in Texas and the Southwest, as well as the eastern US. They also live throughout Florida and the lower Midwest, such as in Missouri.

The red velvet ant is an adorable little insect, about an inch in length, with a thick, velvety reddish-orange-and-black coat of fuzz on the three parts of its body. It almost looks like a small, crawling Mohawked stuffed animal, so soft and brightly colored that you want to reach down and pet it. There's even one species of velvet ant called the panda ant, that owes its name to its fuzzy black-and-white fur. On past scouting trips—when I wasn't looking to get stung— I'd encountered velvet ants that were yellow, and they had an iridescence to them that made them appear almost blue. Whatever the species of velvet ant, their coloring is always aposematic, and they're not aggressive. It's just the opposite, in fact; they usually only sting when people step on them, or when they want nothing more than to get away from predators. In short, these are captivating little creatures that you'd never know could deliver such a potent sting— unless you provoked them, and were unfortunate enough to come in contact with their terrifying stingers.

BODY FUZZ: a brightly colored warning

WINGS: females don't have them

LENGTH: one inch

STINGER: a half inch laced with venom

The red velvet ant's stinger is as long as its abdomen, and it's concealed within the body, so you can't see it unless the bug is attempting to sting. It's needle-sharp and measures nearly half an inch in length...so saying it's intimidating is an understatement. Only the females of the species can sting, and that's because the stinger is a modified ovipositor, which is an organ used for laying eggs. The first time I set eyes on it, going in and out of the insect's abdomen, I cringed at the thought of its enormous stinger penetrating my skin. It was that scary!

The velvet ant is nicknamed the cow killer because it's rumored to have a sting that's so painful it can topple a cow. But I knew this was just an old wives' tale. Trust me, no wasp ever killed a cow unless that animal went into anaphylactic shock or was positively swarmed and stung repeatedly.

Justin Schmidt ranked the sting of the velvet ant as the fourth-most painful insect sting in the world—a three on his chart, with only the warrior wasp, tarantula hawk, and bullet ant above it. He said that the pain from the sting would last an incredible thirty minutes!

DID YOU KNOW?

Female velvet ants are wingless, or apterous, wasps—not ants at all! Mature male velvet ants have wings, but they are not capable of stinging like females are.

But while I was doing some research before my trip, I wondered: *What would the site of the sting* look *like? Had anyone other than Justin experienced it? What was actually going to* happen *to me? I mean, it couldn't be that bad, could it?*

I turned to the internet for answers.

"I wouldn't do that," Mario said to me while we huddled in my office late one night before we left for Arizona. "You know everything you see online about being sick or injured, especially in relation to animals, is ten times worse than it actually is."

But I was not to be deterred, and I kept searching. When a page of images loaded up, I couldn't believe what was in front of me! I beheld a ghastly toe with two white blisters surrounded by raw, swollen flesh. Then I saw a mangled red hand, with the pinkie side twice the size it should be. When I quickly shut down the images and started looking for people's accounts of getting stung, I read sentences like: *I experienced searing pain. I wanted to cut my hand off. It's the worst thing that's* ever *happened to me.* Oh my gosh! Was this what I was in for?

This trip to Arizona would provide the fateful answer to that question.

The reason we decided to look for a velvet ant in Arizona was partially practical. The Brave Wilderness crew aims to film as many animal encounters as we can on a single trip, and we knew from our research that the tarantula hawk and the velvet ant both live in the Sonoran Desert. My mom also lives there, and with its multitude of amazing creatures, wide-open spaces, and great lighting, it never failed to feel both like home *and* a perfect spot for filming. So we settled on spending a few days there and filming two episodes. I knew that accomplishing the velvet ant and the tarantula hawk in the same trip was a tall order, but I'd already encountered some massive insect-driven pain and made it out alive. Handling a few more shouldn't be too bad...except for the fact that these were two of the top four on Justin's list. I was in for more pain than I could have ever imagined.

When we got to the Sonoran Desert and settled in, the crew and I made a plan. We'd go out hunting for the velvet ant in the early mornings and evenings, when it was partially light and a little cool. Female

DID YOU KNOW?

When a velvet ant encounters a threat, it makes a squeaking sound called stridulation by rubbing a specialized scraper on its thorax against a file on its abdomen, causing a high-pitched vibration.

velvet ants scurry quickly along the ground looking for shady spots—old pieces of wood, rocks, debris, or fallen, spine-covered plants—so we knew we wouldn't be able to locate them under the blistering daytime sun. We were going to spend hours and hours turning over rocks, crouching beneath cacti, and looking under rotting logs, and we estimated it would take a few days to find this elusive insect.

Yet, about midway through our second morning out, I turned over a fallen piece of a cholla cactus, and I couldn't believe my eyes.

"Guys, I found one!" I screamed.

Behold! There was a fuzzy, larger-than-average, wingless female red velvet ant scuttling away and trying to avoid a Coyote encounter. I knew I had to catch her fast, before she ran into a burrow or nestled herself into a crevice between cracked pieces of branches, so I chased after her, holding in my hands

a small red-topped container that I'd used to scoop up bugs in a few of the other Brave Wilderness episodes. This canister is actually an old beef bouillon container that my mom had put out with the trash a year or so before. When I saw it, I thought, *That's a perfect bug catcher!* So I cleaned it up, poked a few holes in the top so the insects could breathe, and carried it along with me every time I went insect hunting.

"Are you sure that's a female velvet ant?" Mark asked as he approached me.

"I'm one hundred percent positive," I said. "It's got red-and-black fur and no wings."

Mark broke into big smile and high-fived me. This was it, we had our cow killer! Knowing that the sting portion of the episode was going to take longer to film—and it was going to be blazing hot in a matter of hours—we decided to take a break until the next day.

In any Brave Wilderness episode, the animal is the star of our show—an A-list celebrity as far as we're concerned—and we always want to treat them with the utmost respect. Even though the velvet ant was

Found one!

We have our cow killer!

a stinging beast who might send me to the hospital in less than twenty-four hours, I made a miniature ecosystem for her, putting sand and small plants into her container. When Chance, Mario, Mark, and I sat down to dinner that night, we actually placed that container on the table next to us. In that moment, she was one of the family.

But even with the cow killer hiding under a leaf in a plastic jar, I still felt uncomfortable. I kept thinking: *It's one thing to be stung by a regular old insect like the fire ant, who's been well studied. It's another to be coming stinger-to-skin with an insect so elusive it took me a day and a half to find her!*

A-LIST CELEBRITY

The cow killer is one intimidating foe!

I didn't want to think about her stinger, but I couldn't stop. I went to bed after dinner, images of it curling out of her abdomen swirling around in my brain, and I tossed and turned all night. When I woke up exhausted the next morning, the team and I started to discuss the events of the day.

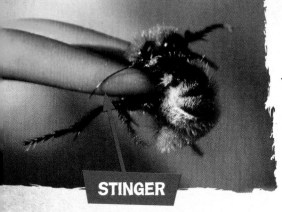
STINGER

"Are you sure you want to go through with this?" Mario asked. "You're not looking so great."

"I have to," I replied. "There's no turning back at this point."

We traveled outside to our controlled environment, EpiPen and forceps tipped with green rubber right in place on the table. I didn't expect to have to use the forceps, though; I'd moved the velvet ant to a glass capsule with a removable wooden bottom, and I thought I'd use it to put the insect on my arm, holding her under the glass till she stung me.

As the cameras began rolling, I upended the capsule on a designated spot on my forearm. Instead of turning to the side and unleashing her stinger, though, the cow killer started scratching and burrowing on the edge of the glass, trying to find an escape. This intelligent little creature bit me repeatedly—*ow!*—as she systematically worked her way around the glass, her long legs digging furiously at the base. We let her do this for a couple of minutes until we realized that the insect was only interested in escaping—*not* stinging.

"Cut," I said. "It's time to activate plan B. Let's use the forceps."

This was as much for the viewer as it was for

The cow killer was only interested in escaping—*not* stinging.

myself. I was practically dying of anticipation, imagining how it would feel when the stinger pierced my skin. Beads of sweat had formed below the brim of my hat, and the glass capsule's interior was getting foggy just from the heat of my skin. I flipped the small containment unit upside down, grasped the entomology forceps between my fingers, and carefully reached in toward the velvet ant.

Even though cow killers have extremely rigid exoskeletons—one of the hardest of any insect—and likely won't be injured even if you step on them, I knew I had to be gentle and exact. If I held her by the head, I might lose her, and if I got her by the abdomen, she could rotate up and sting me before the time was right. As I pulled the bug out of the jar, though, I clearly wasn't holding on to her thorax tightly enough because I lost my grip and she wiggled free. *Plop!* She landed on the table and tried to scurry

The exoskeleton is incredibly tough.

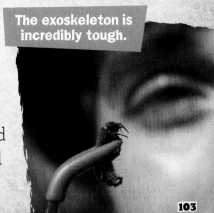

away, but I regained my composure, grabbed her quickly, and got a good, clean hold. Trust me, securing a moving, inch-long target right on the thorax with entomology forceps is much more difficult than it looks!

"Okay, are the cameras set?" I asked. "GoPro is rolling, and I don't want to do this more than once."

"Yup," said Mark. "Rolling."

I took a deep breath. "I'm Coyote Peterson, and I'm about to enter...the Sting Zone...with the cow killer."

The moment of anticipation before the cow killer's stinger touched my flesh was unlike anything I had faced before. Even though I knew there was a very slim chance I would have an allergic reaction and was safe with an EpiPen standing by, I was still petrified. The pain I was about to feel was entirely unknown— and it was going to be something awful.

I waited, my heart pounding, and in a final moment of courage, I thrust the insect down onto my naked arm. Yet the cow killer didn't immediately sting me.

Hmm, I thought, *maybe she doesn't have the right purchase*. I turned the forceps just a little bit, and the insect's abdomen turned to the side. Then I watched as her giant stinger emerged from her body, wrapped around her abdomen, descended toward my skin...and missed me entirely.

Ack! I thought. *I don't know how much more of this I can take!*

It's one thing to feel fear, but it's another thing entirely not to feel that fear release. It's like a balloon that just keeps filling up, stretching and straining, but won't explode. The pressure was too much, and I watched again in horror as the cow killer's stinger slid out of her body and missed me several more times.

Then, suddenly...*whoosh!* The stinger punched into my skin with a lightning-fast prick, and I yelped and dropped the velvet ant on the table. Was I in pain? Not yet. In the two seconds it took me to grab the glass capsule and recontain the insect, I felt almost nothing. Then, as quickly as the surprise of *not* feeling pain hit me, what seemed like a thousand tiny paper cuts sliced into me. The venom had hit my bloodstream, and there was no turning back.

"Oh, wow! Oh, wow! Okay!" I yelled.

The pain was scorching and searing, like someone had laid a red-hot poker on my arm and pressed down. I couldn't stop it, and the sudden, intensely foreign sensation radiated up my arm in hot waves, prickling and tingling my skin as if it was on fire. It kept getting hotter, too, like a fireball shooting through the air at a million miles per hour, growing bigger every second.

I jumped up, grabbed my arm, and began running around.

"Oh my gosh! This is super bad!" I screamed. Somehow, I never said a swear word. This had become one of my trademarks: Even when he's in absolute, unbearable agony, Coyote Peterson doesn't swear!

The pain simmered to a slow boil for five to seven minutes, and then it leveled off to a manageable—yet extreme—degree of discomfort. I could see a lemon-size welt forming

Oh my gosh! This is super bad!

under the skin, and it was expansive but not bright red. It looks solid purple on the footage, but it was actually blotchy red instead of a uniform color. I now know this mottled pattern is because the cow killer's venom is slow-acting as it travels through your blood stream and attacks your body.

After a few minutes, we turned off the cameras. Over the next thirty minutes, the blotchiness extended up my arm in a spiderweb-like fashion, almost as if the blood vessels were bursting under my skin. Red dots then formed, and my arm was hot to the touch, tender, and throbbing. I began to feel a little loopy—whether from the heat of the desert sun or the pain, I can't say. All I know is that I couldn't get my lines right, and I stumbled over my words as we started to film again.

But in the end, Justin Schmidt was right. Thirty minutes after the velvet ant's sting, the pain was entirely gone. It certainly was the most intense sting

I'd ever taken, but when the pain was done, it was done. When I went to bed that night, my arm was slightly itchy and irritated, but it certainly wasn't like the fire ants, whose itchy welts had to be contained under cool, wet towels so I could fall asleep.

Red dots formed, and my arm was hot to the touch, tender, and throbbing.

When the cow killer episode hit the internet a little over a month later, it caught fire in a viral storm of views, and we as a production team couldn't have been happier. "STUNG by a COW KILLER!" collected over a million and a half views in the first twenty-four hours of its release, which set a record for the Brave Wilderness channel. At one point in the first three days of the episode's release, the entire channel went viral and began getting 1.2 million views per hour! This kind of

activity sparked incredible growth on the Brave Wilderness Channel, and in just a single day we even gained three hundred forty-two thousand new subscribers. The results of this video were absolutely staggering, and to date this episode reigns as the most watched video in our library, proudly boasting over forty-three millon views!

Until the day I met the cow killer, I'd suspected what my mission was, but now I knew it: The Coyote Pack was growing, and that was because I'd dramatically raised the stakes for what I could endure. I was midway up the ladder, and I had to climb higher to the next level of Justin Schmidt's insect sting pain index, where I was destined to face the nightmarish wasp known as...the tarantula hawk!

CHAPTER 7

TERROR FROM ABOVE!

TARANTULA HAWK
(PEPSIS THISBE)

PAIN INDEX
4

At the end of every episode I film, I tell the Coyote Pack to be brave—and I always mean it. I'm far from the bravest person in the world, but I've learned a lot about courage through every dangerous, terrifying, and nerve-racking animal encounter I've faced—from putting my arm into an alligator's jaws to allowing slithering, slimy, bloodsucking leeches to attach to my flesh and enjoy a meal. One of the things I now know is that true bravery involves pushing yourself past your comfort zone, to a place that you know is going to be scary. Of course, you need to head into that challenge with your eyes wide open, understanding all the risks involved, but it's important to embrace a healthy amount of fear. After all, conquering the anxiety you feel burning inside you is one of the greatest accomplishments in life.

That's exactly how I looked at my next insect encounter in the days after I'd been stung by the red velvet ant. I'd come to Arizona to meet the tarantula hawk—a gargantuan insect so ferocious that it paralyzes desert tarantulas with just one sting—and

I was going to do it even though I was scared out of my mind. I knew that this massive beast with hooked claws and a venomous, thornlike stinger landed at a four on Justin Schmidt's insect sting pain index, and that assured the most intense pain of my life. But I'd promised the Coyote Pack I'd do it, and I wasn't going to back down. I wanted to be as brave as I told my viewers to be, and that meant I had to muscle through my fears and embrace the courage that would make me stronger.

So, less than two days after the cow killer scuttled out of my glass capsule and back into the Sonoran Desert, I headed outside to hunt for the ruthless, cunning, and brutal tarantula hawk!

———————

The tarantula hawk isn't a bird, and it isn't a spider. Instead, it's one of the 133 species of spider wasps found throughout the Americas. With a dark body that shimmers an iridescent blue in the sun, and paperlike burnt-orange wings that span perpendicular to its thorax, it's over four inches long, making it far and away the largest wasp in the United States. It's so huge, in fact, that when it approaches you—*vroom!*—it's like an Apache helicopter thundering across the blue sky—you can hear it before you see it.

Tarantula hawks are solitary insects, preferring to live alone around flowering trees, which they pollinate. Though my mom once told me that she'd seen about thirty of them perched high in a tree in the Sonoran Desert, the females of the species

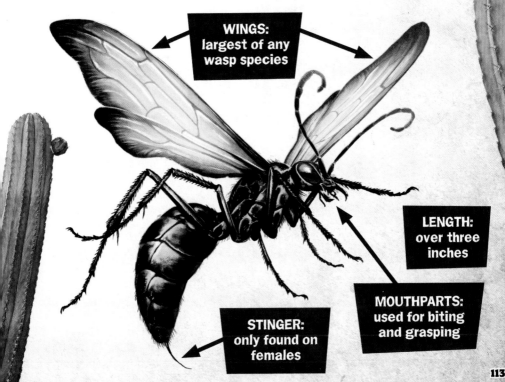

WINGS: largest of any wasp species

LENGTH: over three inches

MOUTHPARTS: used for biting and grasping

STINGER: only found on females

always hunt alone. They're not hunting for their next meal, either; adult tarantula hawks get their nutrition entirely from nectar. Instead, tarantula hawks prey upon—you guessed it—tarantulas, and they do it for the sole purpose of laying their eggs inside the spiders' bodies.

Wait, what? you ask. *Tarantula hawks lay their eggs inside a creature that's up to eight times heavier than they are?* They do, indeed! In one of the most gruesome, brutal, and bizarre reproductive rituals in nature, tarantula hawks lure, attack, paralyze, and then lay their eggs inside these hairy, venomous arachnids.

Female tarantula hawks are intelligent, highly evolved insects, and by sensing a certain chemical, they zero in on a tarantula as it makes its way in and out of the burrow it's built on the desert ground. When the tarantula finally goes inside for good, the wasp swoops down to the burrow and pitter-patters around it till the spider inside thinks it smells lunch. The arachnid then wanders outside, ready to enjoy a hearty

meal of delicious wasp—only to encounter the surprise of its life! The tarantula hawk plants herself between the spider and its safe, secure home, then begins taunting the tarantula by circling it. Desperate to flee, the slower-moving tarantula can't find a way to escape, and it aggressively rears up and bares its fangs. This threat is of no use. Moving one way, then another, the tarantula hawk maneuvers around the spider, approaches, backs off, then charges. *Hi-ya!* In what looks like a black belt–level jujitsu move, the attacking wasp leaps onto the spider and grapples with it, always attempting to gain position by grabbing on with its hooked claws. The tarantula hawk is so fast and cunning that, when she finds an opening, she extends her abdomen under the spider—whose bottom side is softer than its top—and forcefully pushes in her stinger. As a toxic brew shoots out of the stinger into

DID YOU KNOW?

Tarantula hawks sting and paralyze tarantulas, drag them into their own burrow, then lay a single egg on the spider for incubation.

the spider, the poor creature becomes immediately paralyzed. From the onset, it appears to be the makings of an epic battle, but truth be told, it's actually very one-sided. In the words of Dr. Gavin Broad, a British expert on wasps, "the wasps always win. I don't think anyone has ever seen a tarantula kill the wasp."

But it's not over yet! The tarantula hawk then drags the paralyzed spider back into its very own burrow, deposits a single egg in a coating of ooze on top of it, and then closes up the tunnel. While the tarantula is comatose but still alive, the egg matures. When it becomes larva, it pokes a hole in the spider's abdomen and sucks out its vital fluids. Finally, it mercilessly eats the spider's organs from the inside out, killing it. Then, like someone who's eaten way too much turkey and stuffing at Thanksgiving, it lies inside the dead spider's abdomen for a few weeks, goes through metamorphosis, and emerges as a full-grown wasp.

Ack! The whole process is like something from a horror movie, yet I, Coyote Peterson, was going to let this cold-blooded insect sting me!

———————————————————

Mental and physical preparedness are two different

things. I was so nervous that I knew I'd never feel one hundred percent emotionally okay about the prospect of getting stung again so soon, especially by something so much worse than the velvet ant. But at least my body was prepared! After twenty-four hours, all the itchiness, swelling, and redness I'd experienced immediately after the cow killer sting had gone away. I'd also done my research, and I knew that any wasp venom I still had in me wouldn't interact negatively with a new variety.

My research did warn me about the pain I'd feel from the tarantula hawk's massive, quarter-inch stinger, and that was echoed in all the stories I heard. Justin Schmidt compared the sensation to an electrical shock that shoots through your body, rendering you incapable of doing anything except screaming. And my good friend Phil, who lives not far from my mom in Arizona, told me the story of how he'd once fished a tarantula hawk out of his pool, thinking it was dead. When he picked it up to throw it into the brush, it turned around and stung his finger.

"It was the worst pain of my life," he said. "I felt like I'd been Tasered. I couldn't move my fingers for five solid minutes."

Was I really ready for this? I was losing sleep just thinking about it. But I knew that I had to be brave. That meant pushing through my fears, past my comfort zone, and headfirst into one of the greatest challenges of my life.

It was the beginning of August, which is in the middle of the Sonoran Desert's monsoon season. Most people think of the desert as being constantly dry, but that's not the case: All throughout August and September, hundreds of thousands of gallons of water pour from the sky, flooding the parched, dusty

ground. These heavy rains push animals out of their burrows as flowering plants begin to bloom. It's an active time, and with greenery so lush, the tarantula hawk sets about its business pollinating. That's why Mark, Mario, Chance, and I knew we'd have no problem spotting one.

Catching one was another matter, though! Armed with my entomology net, I set out into the desert two mornings after I'd been stung by the cow killer. Within a few hours, I spotted three or four tarantula hawks, and I ran after them, swinging the net trying to swoop them up. But they flew away—loud, fast, and out of sight.

Hours later, as the sun was crossing from the top of the sky on its slow descent toward the horizon, I heard what sounded like a tiny, whirring B-52 bomber approaching. *Brrrrrr*. I turned my head and looked up. There it was! A tarantula hawk, her orange wings blazing against the sky.

I'm going after this one!

"Guys," I whispered, knowing that the wasp, who wants nothing more than to escape from a predator, would dart away in the other direction if she heard me. "I'm going after this one."

The tarantula hawk flew toward the back side of a rocky slope, and I tiptoed after it.

"Careful," Mark said as I scurried down the slope with my net in hand, and I raised my finger to signal that I had my sights on the insect. Then, silently, I dipped out of the crew's line of vision.

Right at the back of the rocks stood an ocotillo, a tall, fingerlike green plant that, despite its name and thick covering of spines, is actually not a cactus at all. The tarantula hawk was clearly interested in the red flowers that had sprouted up because of the heavy rains, and she had landed on the other side of a branch. That branch separated me from the insect I was desperate to catch, and I wasn't sure what to do. But after a handful of failed catches earlier in the day, I knew this might be my last chance.

Go for it, Coyote, I thought.

Because the ocotillo was vertical, the tarantula hawk didn't have a good purchase on it, and she was going to have to reposition herself to take off. As I came around the side of the tall plant, planning to move the branch ever so slightly, the wasp hopped. I knew she was going to have to work up some speed to fly away, so I dove toward her, my net raised. Then I swiped.

Victory! I thought, seeing the wasp trapped inside the net. Then I started shrieking. "Ow! Ack!"

Sure enough, I'd fallen right on top of a cholla cactus! One entire side of my body and my arm was covered in small, spiky cactus balls.

The crew came running at the sound of me screaming, and they were practically speechless when they saw me. But they kept filming as we removed the cactus balls spike by spike. Little did we know then, but that footage would turn into a nice little cactus episode that we used as a teaser for the tarantula hawk. Maybe there isn't such a thing as a mistake?

When the spikes were all out of me, we climbed back up the rocks, and I carefully removed the tarantula hawk from the net and put her inside my modified beef bouillon capsule, sealing it tight. Then we hiked back to our base-camp house, where we had set up a temporary enclosure for the wasp, built with screening and packed full of sticks and greenery. We put the capsule inside, removed the lid, and let the tarantula hawk fly out. Freedom!

Of course, I slept terribly again that night, even worse than I had before the cow killer sting. I kept remembering all the things Justin Schmidt had written, things like: "Blinding, fierce, and shockingly electric...To me, the pain is like an electric wand that hits you, inducing an immediate, excruciating pain."

But I knew I had to power through my fears, so I forced myself into a fitful sleep. When the light broke at the unthinkably early hour of 5:30 AM, I knew it was go time—whether I liked it or not.

By 6:30 AM, we'd safely extracted the wasp from her overnight residency and placed her in a larger glass jar with a tree branch inside, and we trudged out to our film set, which was a solid twenty-minute walk away. The whole time, I could hear the huge insect buzzing inside the container, a steady, static hum, like that of an electric transformer.

Based on our experience with the velvet ant, we knew we probably weren't going to be able to set the capsule on my forearm and induce a sting, so I positioned the entomology forceps nearby. I then reached for the net, set it on the table, put the canister in the net and lifted it up. I tipped it over and watched the hawk emerge. This huge, hulking beast scurried out and entangled herself in the soft confines of the net, and that's when I reached in with the forceps and tried to grab hold.

Getting purchase on an ant is no easy feat, but securing a flying insect is even more challenging. You have to try hard not to damage their delicate

ENTOMOLOGY
FORCEPS

wings, so I placed the forceps right on the bug's thorax, behind where the wings connected to it. I wasn't too worried about damaging the wasp's body— their exoskeleton is so rigid that they can hit people's car windshields and still not splatter—but I did have to expose the abdomen so the tarantula hawk could tilt it and sting me.

With the wasp lightly pinned, I peeled back the folds of the net like layers of an onion, and I descended on the trapped beast with my forceps. I pinched the wasp's thorax, and *boom!* Perfect hold.

> Without a doubt, this is the most intimidating stinger I've ever seen in my life.

"Let's get some shots in case you get stung, you drop it, and it flies away," said Mark.

Easier said than done, I thought. I was so nervous my hand was shaking. As the wasp's legs moved frantically, her mouth chomped up and down, and her abdomen pulsed. I was struggling to catch my breath, and I had to do my best not to drop the forceps and run.

The tarantula hawk's stinger was moving in and out this whole time, and it was the first time I'd seen it up close. It was jet-black and massive—about a quarter of an inch in length—and it had a slight curve

to it. It was much thicker than the velvet ant stinger,
like a thorn off a rose. *Without a doubt, this is the most
intimidating stinger I've ever seen in my life*, I said to
myself as my palms started to sweat.

I lay the massive wasp down on my forearm,
forceps still tight, and I waited. The tarantula hawk's
abdomen squirmed back and forth, and I could feel
her mandibles biting my skin. I shifted the forceps just
a little bit so the thorax was more exposed, and, then...

BOOM!

A lightning bolt struck my arm as the stinger
went into my flesh.
Unlike the velvet
ant's stinger, which
felt like a slippery,
lubricated needle as
it went in and out of
my skin, the tarantula

Ugh...ugh...
ugh...ugh!

hawk's sting was like being jabbed by an electrified sword.

"Ugh...ugh...ugh...ugh!" I moaned as the wasp tumbled onto the table. I have no idea how I had the presence of mind to do it, but I quickly encapsulated the wasp under the glass and got her back under control. Then I fell onto the ground, screaming in agony as my hand seized up into a state of paralysis.

The pain was so searing that I lost track of time for almost five minutes. It radiated up my arm in hot, electric waves that peaked at minute five. Then the

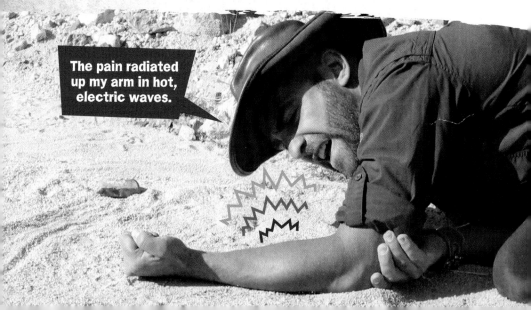

The pain radiated up my arm in hot, electric waves.

pain started to lessen and I could feel the venom seeping out from the site of the sting. I knew my immune system was responding in full gear.

My hand began to relax, and I moved my fingers just to be sure my arm wasn't paralyzed. As I stood up, I could see a lemon-size welt beginning to form on my arm, just as I'd gotten with the velvet ant. My forearm was tender and bright red, and I could see an area of

My skin felt like sandpaper when touched.

blotchiness developing. Soon, raised bumps popped up on my skin that felt like sandpaper when touched.

Within ten minutes, I began feeling like myself again, and I was able to go back in front of the camera to present the sting. What looked like a water balloon formed under my skin several hours later, and my entire forearm swelled up and began to itch terribly. But two days later, it all passed. The most intense

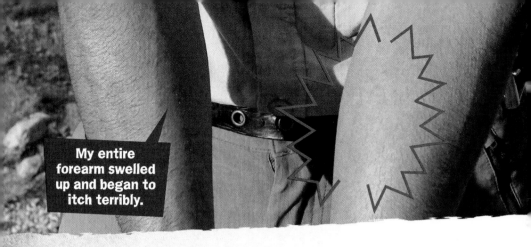

My entire forearm swelled up and began to itch terribly.

sting of my life—made all the more dramatic by the demented horror story of the paralyzing wasp and my thrown-to-the-ground-in-agony roll-around—was soon a distant memory.

We knew that we had lightning in a bottle with this episode, and while at that point in time the velvet ant episode was still to be released, it was a combination of both that set the stage for taking on the next level of Justin Schmidt's insect sting pain index...the bullet ant challenge. Facing the tarantula hawk definitely

Facing the tarantula hawk definitely pushed me past my comfort zone.

pushed me past my comfort zone, but I had faced my fears and taken the sting.

To date, "STUNG by a TARANTULA HAWK!" boasts a staggering thirty-eight million views and seems always to be the video that viewers can't believe we filmed. The alien nature of this fascinating insect, the story that paints a horrifying picture of its reproductive behaviors, and the power of its electric sting make it a fan favorite. Personally, I am very proud of this episode. Not for its collection of views or its fantastic production value, but because so many people learned about this often-misunderstood creature. My goal is always, first and foremost, to educate the audience, and I think more people now know about the tarantula hawk than ever before.

CHAPTER 8

THE BEE BEARD BLUNDER!

HONEY BEE
(APIS MELLIFERA)

PAIN INDEX
2

LOCATION: ARIZONA, USA

Everybody has their favorite part of the circus—whether it's seeing a daredevil on a motorcycle racing around a spherical cage that's engulfed in flames, or watching an animal trainer stand in front of an angry lion, the animal's teeth and claws bared as he rears up in a display of power. These are moments of danger that test a viewer's nerves as much as the person who's committing the act. For the Coyote Pack, these kinds of edge-of-your-seat episodes have been the most beloved. But every show needs a clown for comic relief—someone to take the pressure off a scary scene—and that's exactly what the Brave Wilderness crew and I were going for when we decided that I should re-create a bee beard in February 2017. *We can teach the world about honey bees* and *get a few laughs*, we thought. *It's a win-win!*

Little did we know, though, that the bee beard episode would become one of our most jaw-droppingly dangerous and painful insect encounters ever!

For those of you not familiar with a bee beard, let me explain it to you. A bee beard is just what it sounds like: A person (in this case, me) allows a beekeeper to place a colony of honey bees on their cheeks, upper lip, chin, and neck, creating a full, buzzing beard. Sometimes the bees cover the person's eyes and mouth, and other times they extend over their head and down their back. If you've ever seen photos of bee beards, the people wearing them usually look positively happy, like it's no big deal to have thousands and thousands of bees swarming their face. Many who have had the experience even say it's a load of fun!

After my experience with the bee beard, though, I can very much assure you this was not the case for me. Honey bees aren't toys; they're complicated creatures that warrant caution and deserve our respect.

Over the course of 2016, the Brave Wilderness crew had filmed me getting stung by countless terrifying venomous ants and two incredibly powerful wasps, yet we hadn't talked about one of nature's most common stinging insects: the honey bee. I knew how important bees are to the environment—they're the most prolific pollinators in the world—so I couldn't wait to get up close and personal with nature's little helpers, especially if I got a chance to have a bee beard! Since I was a kid, they'd always seemed fun and quirky, and I

knew the Coyote Pack would get a kick out of seeing me with one. So Mark, Mario, and I decided to travel to a bee sanctuary called Life'Sweet Honey Farms, in Tucson, Arizona, to film an episode with our friend Chris Brinton, who's one of the Southwest's most well-respected bee experts.

"It'll be a piece of cake," Chris said when we got there. "These bees are totally docile, and you're not going to get stung."

Justin Schmidt had ranked the western honey bee as a two on the insect sting pain index, saying that any discomfort lasted only ten minutes. I'd been stung by bees several times in my life, so I

DID YOU KNOW?
European honey bees can communicate with one another by using chemicals called pheromones to create signals!

knew this was true. The sting consists of a sharp prick, some momentary burning, and then a large amount of localized swelling—caused by a particular neurotoxin—that goes away within a day or two. I wasn't afraid of bees, and as far as I knew I wasn't allergic to them, so I assumed I could handle the bee beard. Besides, I wasn't going to get stung, right?

DID YOU KNOW?
The science of beekeeping is called apiculture.

"All your viewers are going to be disappointed," Chris joked. "The first insect episode where Coyote Peterson doesn't get stung!" Everyone laughed, including me. Whether or not the honey bees attacked me didn't matter; this episode was comedic relief with an educational component. Maybe the episode wouldn't be very dramatic, but no one really cared because learning about bees was our true goal.

We had no cause to believe the western honey bees Chris and his crew kept at the bee sanctuary would be aggressive because this type of bee only attacks when their hives are threatened. We wouldn't be doing that. The situation was quite the opposite, in fact. Chris and his crew are bee conservationists, and they'd rescued this particular colony from someone's house the day before. They'd used a vacuum system that was a thousand times more sophisticated than my little Bug Sucker 5000, and they planned to use the bees for honey production. I'd had Chris's granular golden honey before, and it was without a doubt the most delicious honey I had ever eaten. It was instant, pure energy, and I even planned to take a few jars home with me after the shoot so I could share with friends and family.

The western honey bee is also called the European honey bee, and it's one of the approximately twenty

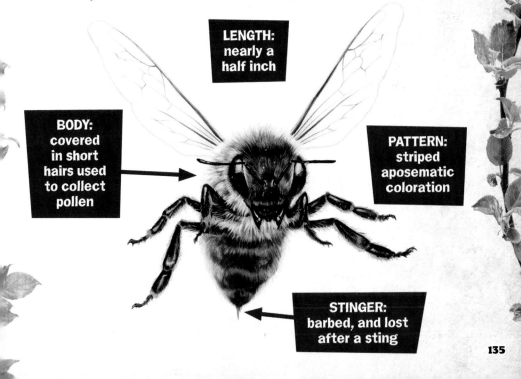

LENGTH:
nearly a
half inch

BODY:
covered
in short
hairs used
to collect
pollen

PATTERN:
striped
aposematic
coloration

STINGER:
barbed, and lost
after a sting

subspecies of honey bee that are found on every continent except Antarctica. They're indigenous to Europe, Africa, and the Middle East, but thanks to humans, who learned quickly how effective these bees are at pollinating, they're now found in all the temperate regions of the earth.

Like most species of bees, western honey bee hives are populated by three categories of bees: queens, workers, and drones. There's only one queen bee in a colony, and she's the sole reproductive member. Usually only about three-quarters of an inch long, she's still the biggest in the hive, with a fatter, longer abdomen than everyone else. When the queen was larva, she was exclusively fed a diet of something called royal jelly, a milky-white substance that's a rich combination of water, proteins, and sugars. After going through metamorphosis and emerging as an adult bee, she then spends the rest of her life laying eggs in the waxy cells of the honeycomb, many of which have been fertilized by drones.

There's only one queen bee in a colony, and she's the sole reproductive member.

Drones are the males of the hive, and they're typically only slightly smaller than the queen, with a thinner abdomen. Their distinguishing features are their eyes, which are black, round, large, and touch each other at the top center of their heads. Interestingly, drones develop from unfertilized eggs, and they don't have stingers. They don't really need them because they don't defend the hive. Their only purpose is to fertilize the queen bee, which they do in flight. Then, immediately after fertilization, the drones die.

As I said, queen bees lay eggs inside the combs, some of which are fertilized and some of which aren't. The fertilized eggs, like the unfertilized, are fed pollen and nectar, and they develop into worker bees. Worker bees are all female, and their bodies are smaller than both queens and drones. They serve two purposes: First, they help build up the wax comb inside the hive

Worker bees are all female, and their bodies are smaller than both queens and drones.

using wax scales on the underside of their abdomens. Second, they leave the nest and gather pollen and nectar on structures called pollen baskets, which are situated on their back legs. Like queen bees, they have stingers, but their stingers have barbs, so an attack causes their venom sac to rip out and leads to their almost-immediate death.

These stinging worker bees were the ones I was going to be coated by, but I didn't need to worry about anything. I wasn't going to be stung, was I? No way. Chris had assured me, and the way his crew was dressed proved it.

A lot of times when you see beekeepers, they're wearing protective suits that cover them head to toe, with a wire mask that covers their faces and heads. When Chris's crew moved toward the colony of bees, they were just wearing gloves, and only the man that got the bees out of their enclosure was wearing a mask. Chris approached me with what looked like a cocktail straw filled with a light-green liquid. He explained that this glowstick-like contraption was called a pseudo queen, and it was a gluten compound that mimicked

PROTECTIVE SUITS

the pheromones a queen bee emits. The worker bees
would sense it when they got close to me, and it would
lure them right onto my face and neck. He taped the
pseudo queen just below my chin, then turned around
to retrieve the bees. Less than a minute later, he walked
back to me with a tray full of buzzing worker bees in
one hand and a dustpan in the other. He transferred the
bees to the dustpan, placed it just below my neck, and
within seconds, a few flew onto my neck and shirt.

This isn't so bad, I thought. *A little weird, but not bad!*

Within fifteen seconds, though, I was a honey bee
magnet! Hundreds of bees began swarming my neck
and face, their legs tickling me while a steady buzz
rang in my ears. The reality of the situation started to
sink in, and it did *not* feel good. *Oh my gosh,* I thought,
I'm helpless! In truth, I wasn't. I had two EpiPens in my
pocket and could jump up and down anytime I wanted
to get rid of the bees. But I worried that any false move
was going to make them start stinging me. Chris had
also put Vaseline near my eyes, nose, and ears so the
bees couldn't crawl inside me, but my lips were bare.
At about thirty seconds in, one bee scurried onto my

lip when I started talking. I pursed, trying to shoo it away. That clearly freaked out the bee...and then the bee beard started to go wrong!

"*Oww*. Stung on the lip!" I muttered as best I could.

Getting stung on a place that's as sensitive as your lips is never fun, but it didn't hurt that much. I tried to reassure myself that all was well—especially because Chris still seemed so relaxed as he continued piling bees onto my neck. A few times, he raised his gloved hand to my face and slathered the bees on my cheeks like peanut butter on a slice of bread. He'd explained earlier that bees emit a location pheromone that attracts other bees, so I knew that pretty soon he wouldn't need to touch me; more and more would climb on, faster and faster, simply because they sensed the other bees.

Oww. Stung on the lip!

I wasn't supposed to get stung!

I couldn't see it, but at that point I had about three thousand bees on me. And even though Chris seemed cool as a cucumber, the bees weren't. Something had made them angry, and they were about to take it out on Coyote Peterson!

"I'm getting stung a lot!" I mumbled at about the one-minute mark. "I've been stung about six times!"

I couldn't see it on Chris's face, but he must have known something was off. Six stings? That was six more than he said I'd get! Another minute passed, and I could feel the bees crawling on my ears, stinging me en masse. Then one climbed onto my lip and stung me in the exact same place as I'd had the first sting.

OUCHHHH!

Two and a half minutes in, I'd had enough. I could feel sharp, sudden, stinging pain on my ears, neck, arms, and all over my face and lips, and I just couldn't take it anymore. A piece of cake? *Bwah!* I was a human pincushion.

Chris instructed me to jump, and then he and his

guys walked over to me with a can of bug spray and some sort of cloudy white substance that they misted through the air like baby powder. It sent the bees flying off me, scattering them in all directions. I could still feel them on my arms, face, and neck, though, and I knew there were stingers embedded in my ears. What had I done to deserve this? Had I talked too much or moved the wrong way while the bees were piling on?

Later, after we'd counted thirty-two stings on my face, neck, and arms, after my lips had swelled into what looked like two overly plumped hot dogs, and after I'd drooled on camera while trying to describe the pain to my viewers, I learned that getting stung by a horde of bees who were supposed to be docile was not my fault at all! The Coyote Peterson who would spend forty-eight hours looking like some sort of ghoulish Mr. Potato Head had been a victim of Africanized honey bees, also known as killer bees.

Chris and his crew speculated that the hive they'd

used for my bee beard had been invaded by Africanized honey bees, an invasive species that's now spread all over the United States. These bees must have started fighting with the Western bees, and as each type became more and more aggressive against each other, their natural reaction was to sting the first thing they could. That, of course, would be my face!

Africanized honey bees were brought to Brazil from Africa in 1956 for the purpose of increasing honey production. But while a few colonies were being kept in quarantine, the Africanized bees escaped. They swarmed into the surrounding cities and countryside, and then they spent the next twenty-plus years populating every inch of South and Central America. By 1985, they'd made their way up to the United States, and now they live and reproduce throughout

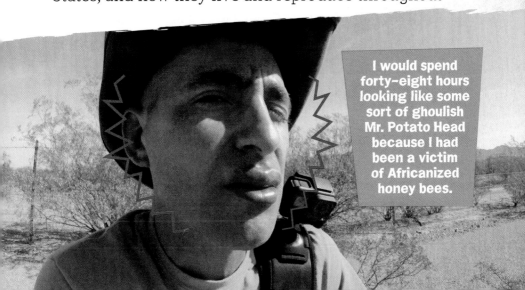

I would spend forty-eight hours looking like some sort of ghoulish Mr. Potato Head because I had been a victim of Africanized honey bees.

AFRICANIZED HONEY BEE

the southwestern United States and South Florida, with many more discovered in additional states every year.

Africanized honey bees are hard to tell apart from Western honey bees, and that's because they're not a different species. They're in fact a subspecies of the Western honey bee, and their only distinguishing physical features are a

EUROPEAN HONEY BEE

slightly smaller size and a few key variations in their wings. What truly sets them apart, though, is their behavior. Africanized honey bees are much more territorial and aggressive than Western honey bees.

While Western honey bees attack in groups of ten or so if their hive is under threat, Africanized honey bees swarm. I don't mean in groups of thirty or forty, either; I'm talking packs of hundreds, if not thousands, of bees that make their way across the blue sky like a giant black tornado. These swarms are estimated to have killed about a thousand people—but whether that's from the sheer number of stings or allergic reactions, I can't say. Regardless, that's how they got their nickname, "killer bees." This term is a bit of a misnomer, though, because their venom is slightly less potent than Western honey bee venom.

I wasn't laughing at the time, but sixteen million views later, the bee beard episode has provided a lot of comic relief. More than that, it's taught millions of Coyote Pack members about the behavior of honey bees and how, despite the relative harmlessness of their stings, they should always be treated with respect. When people ask me if I'd do a bee beard again, my answer is a resounding *NO*. In fact, I'm now super cautious of bees. So much venom poured into me during the bee beard episode that there's a possiblity I've developed an allergy to bee venom, and a single sting could send me into anaphylactic shock. I don't fool around with bees, and neither should you. Admire them from a safe distance, enjoy their delicious honey, and celebrate the wonderful things they do for our planet!

CHAPTER 9

THE BULLET ANT CHALLENGE!

BULLET ANT
(PARAPONERA CLAVATA)

PAIN INDEX
4

In life, there are moments you've been anticipating for what feels like forever. These are occasions you've strived for and built up to with such excitement that, when they're finally about to happen, you can hardly believe it. Your very identity is embodied in moments such as these, so you might be tempted to feel as if you can't do it...that you need to back down because you're just too scared. You're standing at the edge of a cliff, bungee cords secured, ready to jump, but you're petrified! That's when you need to return to your preparation. Know you've trained for this and understand that you're ready. With that supreme self-assuredness, I promise you can do anything!

In the days before being stung by the bullet ant, there were times I thought I wasn't going to make it. I was so nervous, waking up at night in a feverish sweat, worried about the pain I was going to feel when I faced the undisputed champion of the insect sting pain index. Harvester and fire ants had swarmed me with an onslaught of painful and unforgettable stings. The cow killer's attack had been scorching, making me feel as if I'd dipped my forearm into a vat of molten lead. The tarantula hawk's stinging punch had been horrific, knocking me to the ground and causing my arm to seize up for a full five minutes. Could I take any more of this? I knew I had to for the sake of the Coyote Pack, but would it be too much for me?

Of course it wouldn't—because I was ready. I'd endured enough potent insect venom to prepare me for the most brutal sting in the world. Ranked at level four on the insect sting pain index, with the pain lasting an estimated three hundred minutes, I knew I might feel as if I'd been run over by a truck. But I could do it because I, Coyote Peterson, had trained for this.

We had been teasing the idea of being stung by

a bullet ant since the release of our harvester ant episode in the early months of 2016. This sparked an unprecedented amount of encouragement and, honestly, challenging dares from the Coyote Pack, filling the YouTube comment boards. We knew we had to do it, and when the conceptual design of climbing up Justin Schmidt's insect sting pain index became a reality, the Brave Wilderness team and I got to work

RAIN FOREST

immediately, plotting when and where we could encounter this terrifying tropical creature. Mario then unearthed a contact he had in western Costa Rica, where we'd filmed many of our most popular episodes, and *that* friend said he knew someone near the east coast who had a private reserve that was crawling with infamous bullet ants.

Much less developed than its Pacific coast, the Caribbean side of Costa Rica is densely sloped in lush tropical rain forests, the perfect habitat for various insect species including the painfully toxic ant we sought. So Mario called up Brian, the owner of the reserve we aimed to visit, and he was excited about the idea of us coming down to film.

"I'm one hundred percent sure we have bullet ants

here," he said. "In fact, I saw a few just the other day. I can send you some photos."

He did just as he promised, and with hesitant excitement, Mario and I confirmed their identities. *Boom.* This was it! We had without question found a population of bullet ants, so we booked our flights and prepared to film the most highly anticipated episode of our careers.

When we arrived in northeastern Costa Rica in early December 2016, we could hardly believe our eyes. Brian lived and worked on over one hundred ten pristine acres of protected rain forest that were intricately laced with streams and covered by a rich canopy of jungle foliage. On his land lived a plethora of amazing species, including dazzling glass frogs, elusive ocelots, and deadly venomous fer-de-lance vipers. There were also colonies of bullet ants! Brian assured us that we'd have to scour the rain forest floor carefully—cutting through overgrowth and trudging through mud—to find one, but it wouldn't

DID YOU KNOW?
In Venezuela, the local name for the bullet ant translates to "twenty-four-hour ant" because the pain from its sting typically lasts twenty-four hours.

take more than a day or two. The nests were often hidden, but with the right knowledge of where to look, it was only a matter of time. We were still nervous, though; we wanted to get the bullet ant episode out by Christmas, and that meant we only had a few weeks to travel, search, film, edit, and release the content on YouTube. A few weeks may sound like a lot of time to you, but we usually take months to create an episode of this magnitude. In our book, this was lightning-fast.

Bullet ants aren't just found in Costa Rica; their population stretches from the rain forests of Central America through the top half of South America, particularly in and around the Amazon River. This ferocious insect has become the stuff of legend in many parts of those regions, and it plays an important role in the culture of the Sateré-Mawé tribe of Brazil. When the tribe's boys are on the cusp on manhood,

they're sent out into the rain forest to collect as many ants as they can. When they return, a medicine man mixes the colony in an herbal solution, putting them to sleep. Then he sews a dozen or so ants stinger-first inside gloves that are made of palm fronds. The young men stand in a group around a fire, put on the gloves, and then the angry ants wake up! Twenty times over the course of eleven hours, the boys dance blindfolded around a fire, getting stung repeatedly. No boy is considered a warrior till he can make it through the gruesome ritual.

The poneratoxin that makes up the bullet ant's venom is thirty times more potent than bee venom, making it—you guessed it—thirty times more painful. But it also acts as a hallucinogen, so not only do the young Sateré-Mawé men experience paralysis, swelling, and excruciating stinging and burning, but they also become disoriented and hallucinate. Can you imagine getting stung again and again and again, twenty times for half the day? Just the thought of it is enough to make you lose your mind! But I realized the tribe was onto something. For me, the bullet ant sting was a test of courage, and that's the philosophy I had to embrace.

In Costa Rica, the ant is known as *Bala*, which means "bullet" in Spanish. That's not because these creatures can be anywhere from three-quarters to one and a quarter inches, which is about the size of a bullet, or because they're almost metallic black in appearance, with a rusty, iridescent red on their abdomens. It's because people liken the pain from their stings to being shot by a bullet. Looking at a bullet ant close-up,

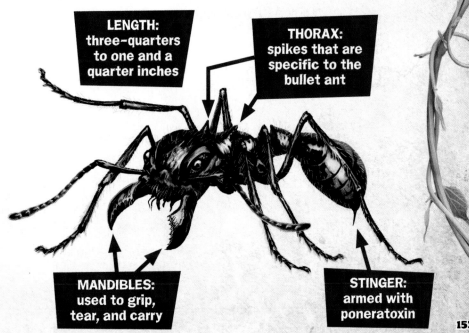

LENGTH: three-quarters to one and a quarter inches

THORAX: spikes that are specific to the bullet ant

MANDIBLES: used to grip, tear, and carry

STINGER: armed with poneratoxin

though, you might be surprised that they can inflict such horrific pain. Sure, they have giant mandibles that open and close like vise grips, but their curved stingers are hidden within their abdomens until the ant feels threatened. Their body parts are also alien-like and incredibly menacing-looking, as if they come together to make up an invader from outer space rather than an insect.

The morning Mark, Mario, and I set out into the rain forest, we knew we had to be careful. The forest floor is full of dangers like venomous snakes, thorny branches, and strange pockets of sink mud that can nearly swallow a human alive. When it came to bullet ants, Brian had seen a few nomadic individuals the week we'd emailed him, so he wasn't much help in pointing us in the right direction of an actual nest. We were going to have to hunt and scour the rain forest to find one, so that is exactly what we did.

For several days, we searched the jungle until finally...success! We found a nest beneath a massive towering tree that seemed to reach all the way into the sky. There, on the forest floor, right at our feet, was the entrance—

DID YOU KNOW?
A bullet ant colony can have up to 2,500 members.

one of several holes, all of which looked as if they'd been dug out by moles rather than ants. I moved my fists toward the ground and started pounding gently, and about ten ants spilled out.

Soldier ants formed a defensive perimeter around the nest's entrance.

Prrrrr. As they left the hole, they were buzzing! Then they spun around and formed a perimeter around the entrance of the colony. Like little guard dogs, they were trying to block us from getting in.

Wow, I thought. *These sure are smart insects! They're setting perimeters, like they're a human military force.*

I grabbed the red-topped bouillon cube container I'd used in so many other episodes, unscrewed the lid, and readied myself to make a catch. I grabbed a branch and carefully stuck it into one of the entrance holes. My goal was to carefully coax the biggest ant I could find inside the container. One ant ran up close to me, and I lured her onto the stick, then tried to place her in the container. Suddenly... attack! The ants that had been standing guard swarmed all around me, and I dropped the container when one deployed from a tree limb onto my hand.

In sheer panic, I flicked off the ant. We all lunged backward and away from the nest—things were getting out of control! We regained our composure, shook ourselves off as best we could, and returned carefully to the tree to reattempt our capture of an ant. The danger was on another level, as this was the most heart-racing insect catch I had ever attempted.

I held my breath and leaned toward the ground, reaching down with the stick. I got one on the tip. The insect, in full attack mode, began biting the wooden tool. This was my chance to get her away from the nest and into the container. I set down the stick on the ground, the ant crawled off, and I placed the plastic capsule in front of the scurrying ant. In storybook fashion, she magically walked right inside. I quickly secured the top, and we exploded in celebration.

"Whoo-hoo, I got it!" I turned to Mario and Mark, who had wide smiles on their faces. We were all

It's impossible not to be intimidated by these fearless, giant stinging ants.

strangely excited, considering that I was mere moments away from being stung by the insect with the most painful sting in the world.

We had identified a great spot in the jungle, near a small research station, where we could film the actual sting. So we set up a table and prepared to get the remainder of the scene. I carefully transferred our angry star from the plastic container into a small glass capsule, where we took time to film B-roll shots and admire her features. The ant was incredible, with a shimmering exoskeleton, sturdy, bristly-haired body, and curved, jagged mandibles. She seemed to be the perfect specimen of bullet ant.

"You're about to be a very famous little ant," I told the insect off camera. "But first, I need you to give me a good solid performance and unforgettable sting so we can educate the world about your incredible abilities."

When the cameras started rolling, I lowered the ant onto my arm in the glass container I'd transferred her to. When she landed on my flesh, her immediate interest was getting used to her strange surroundings

and looking for a way out. About thirty seconds
into filming, the heat from my body began to fog
up the glass, so we changed tactics and went to the
entomology forceps. With quick precision I grabbed
hold of the ant's thorax and successfully got her under
control. *Holy cow*, I thought. *This ant is immediately
going into attack mode!* The aggressive creature's
mandibles moved back and forth, closing like a pair
of pruning shears, while her stinger moved in and out
attempting to sting anything that was foolish enough
to come within range. Now, I'd seen some big stingers
in my life, especially on the velvet ant, but this was a
different level of horror. The stinger was like a sharp
saber, ready to pierce my arm. Was I scared? Of course
I was! My heart was racing, and beads of sweat had
formed on my forehead. But like the warrior I wanted

to become, I'd prepared. I was as full of courage as I'd ever be, and there was no turning back now.

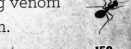
Was I scared? Of course I was!

I looked to the camera, right down the lens, and addressed the Coyote Pack with my classic pre-sting delivery of "I'm Coyote Peterson, and I'm about to enter the Sting Zone with...the bullet ant!" My hands trembling, I placed the ant down on my arm, holding her tight against my flesh. One...two...three...four...five seconds passed...and *pow!* The bullet ant stung me, the stinger thrusting into my body like a lightning bolt. The shock of the force was reminiscent of the tarantula hawk's sting—like being hit by a flaming freight train at full speed—and I dropped the forceps.

"Oh, it's stuck in my arm!" I screamed. "It's stuck in my arm!"

Sure enough, the ant's massive stinger was embedded so deeply in my flesh that it wouldn't come out and was now stuck there, defensively pumping venom into my bloodstream.

By the time I had the presence of mind to reach for the forceps, the ant had finally gained some purchase on my arm, curled her abdomen, and slipped out her stinger, as though she had removed a hook from a fish's mouth.

The fact that the stinger was out made no difference to me, though. The pain accelerated like a rocket ship blasting off. *Whoosh!* The initial explosion of intense fire escalated, and I felt as if my whole arm was being branded by a hot poker, red-hot metal pressing down onto my melting flesh. There wasn't a crescendo of pain, followed by a release, either. The agony was nonstop, and when I threw myself onto the ground

It feels like my arm is on fire!

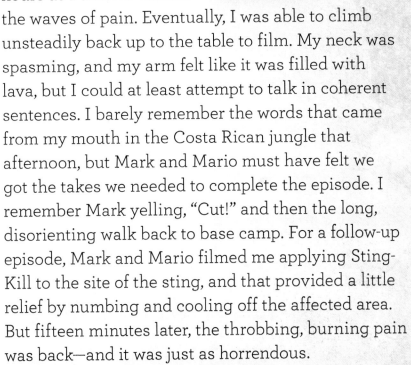

and began rolling around, I was only looking for some sort of distraction from the never-ending fire that had engulfed me.

Minutes seemed like hours as I tried to absorb the waves of pain. Eventually, I was able to climb unsteadily back up to the table to film. My neck was spasming, and my arm felt like it was filled with lava, but I could at least attempt to talk in coherent sentences. I barely remember the words that came from my mouth in the Costa Rican jungle that afternoon, but Mark and Mario must have felt we got the takes we needed to complete the episode. I remember Mark yelling, "Cut!" and then the long, disorienting walk back to base camp. For a follow-up episode, Mark and Mario filmed me applying Sting-Kill to the site of the sting, and that provided a little relief by numbing and cooling off the affected area. But fifteen minutes later, the throbbing, burning pain was back—and it was just as horrendous.

Over the next thirty hours, I experienced massive swelling of my forearm, and I couldn't resist the urge to scratch. I also couldn't make myself comfortable in bed that night, and every time I started to drift off, I was jolted back awake by the sound of my heartbeat in my ears—*pump-pump, pump-pump, pump-pump*. With

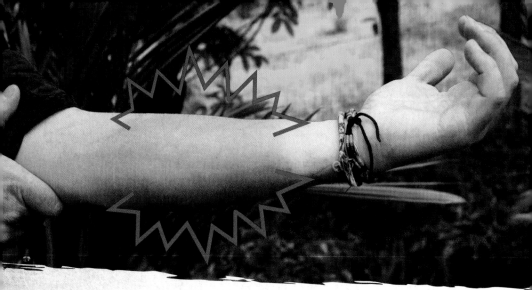

my arm still red and swollen, I decided to get up and get a wet washcloth, which I stuck in the freezer until it was almost frozen and then wrapped around my throbbing arm to alleviate the pain. Unfortunately, it didn't help me much that night. It was a full thirty-six hours after the initial sting—well into the following evening—before I finally felt a sense of relief.

Now that I'm well past the bullet ant challenge and can really think about it, the long, intense duration of my suffering may have had to do with the force of the ant's fiery, electric sting. The initial shock of pain was a blunt force trauma, like a high-speed car wreck, and my muscles tensed up because of it. When I'd been squirming and writhing on the ground, perhaps I'd been like the Sateré-Mawé boys as they danced, attempting to loosen and stretch their muscles so they didn't seize up. My body was in shock, and no matter how brave I felt afterward for accomplishing

this mammoth task, I was still anxious, tense, and traumatized. Something internal that I couldn't put into words had happened, and it was going to take me a long, long time to recover. In fact, for weeks after, I was exhausted.

When we got home on a Friday night, the battle wasn't complete because there was still work to be done. We drove straight from the airport to our office and met our senior editor, Chris. We downloaded the footage, headed home to get a few hours' sleep, and by 6:00 the next morning, we were back at work. Chris edited for forty-eight hours straight, and we released the "STUNG by a Bullet Ant" episode on Tuesday, December 20, just before Christmas, exactly as we'd promised the Coyote Pack we would.

When you climb a mountain, you are going to suffer. But in the end, reaching the summit is entirely

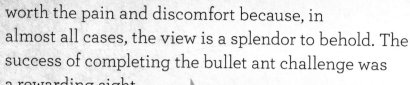

worth the pain and discomfort because, in almost all cases, the view is a splendor to behold. The success of completing the bullet ant challenge was a rewarding sight unlike anything we had ever seen on the Brave Wilderness channel. Within

its first hour on YouTube, the episode had collected more views than we'd ever experienced before, and in three hours' time, a whopping one million eyes had watched it. We'd set a new channel record! To date, the episode boasts a staggering thirty-eight million views and is far and away our most famous episode. It's almost impossible for me to go out in public or sit in an interview and not have someone ask, "Hey, aren't you that guy who got stung by the giant ant?" or "Tell us about getting stung by the bullet ant. Was it really like being shot with a bullet?"

By the end of the year 2016, Brave Wilderness had grown to five million subscribers, and that was all because I'd summoned my courage, come face-to-face with the bullet ant, and then conquered the height of the insect sting pain index. The views and new members

to our channel were certainly rewards in their own rights, but what truly made me happy—the real payoff—was that people around the world were learning about bugs!

In my mind, the climb was over, but as is often the case with mountains, there is always another peak. Sure, we'd given the Coyote Pack what they'd asked for, but I'd left one stinging insect on the list: a wasp Justin Schmidt rumored may be more painful than the ant I had just faced, and was also ranked as a four on his scale. Would Coyote ever come forearm-to-stinger with the legendary warrior wasp? The audience was demanding to see it. Could I let them down? Not a chance. So the team and I set course to face the ultimate warrior!

CHAPTER 10

THE ULTIMATE WARRIOR!

WARRIOR WASP
(SYNOECA SEPTENTRIONALIS)

PAIN INDEX
4

Never let it be said that Coyote Peterson isn't true to his word. I believe that honesty is a testament to your character, so I try to be straightforward and precise in all parts of my life. That's why, when I committed to climbing the insect sting pain index all the way to its peak, I couldn't back down. Doing so would be breaking my solemn vow! And with the Coyote Pack asking me to endure the sting of the warrior wasp, I couldn't let them down. The warrior wasp is ranked as a number four on the insect sting pain index, making it the most potent paper wasp venom in the world. Sure, I knew it was going to deliver a tidal wave of pain, but it was the one final challenge I had no choice but to face!

The Brave Wilderness crew and I knew very little about the warrior wasp when we first heard about it in the comment section of many of our popular sting episodes. Once we began digging, though, we quickly realized how fascinating this creature was, both in terms of its exotic appearance and its aggressive, territorial behavior.

Warrior wasps are a form of paper wasp. They're beautiful insects, with a jet-black exoskeleton that shimmers iridescent blue in the light. Their tear-shaped abdomen is perfectly aerodynamic and pointed at the tip. The exoskeleton is so tightly wrapped around the abdomen that it boasts an almost muscular appearance, as if the insect is wearing a super-hero suit. The wasp's head is pointed, giving it a sharp, predatory appearance, and its mandibles are massive and tinged with a shiny red hue. The point at which the thorax connects to the abdomen is incredibly narrow, making it look as sleek and fast as a fighter jet plane. At around three-quarters of an inch, the warrior wasp isn't the biggest wasp of its species—in fact, it's only

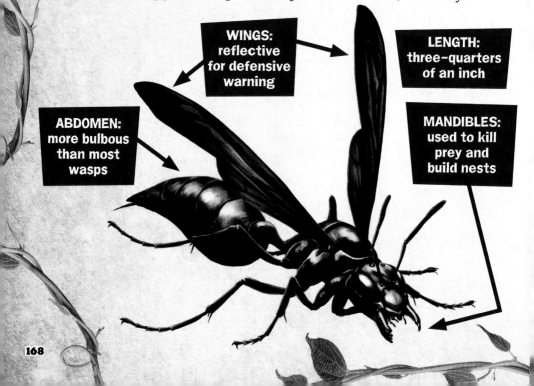

WINGS: reflective for defensive warning

LENGTH: three-quarters of an inch

ABDOMEN: more bulbous than most wasps

MANDIBLES: used to kill prey and build nests

a third the size of the tarantula hawk—but without a doubt, it was the most alien-like wasp I'd ever encountered.

Warrior wasps, like bullet ants, are found in the rain forests of Central and South America, which at first may make you wonder why I hadn't tried to catch one when I was in Costa Rica the winter before. Truth

COSTA RICA

be told, we had no idea these wasps lived within the same range as the bullet ant, and had we played our cards right, we could have gotten both the bullet ant and the warrior wasp on the original trip! As they say, hindsight is 20/20. Then I really stop and think about it: *Bullet ant and warrior wasp back to back?! Give me a break!* There was no possible way! The bullet ant had left me exhausted, psychologically depleted, and physically sore for days. Sure, I wouldn't have died if I'd gotten stung by two level-four insects on the same trip, but it would have been far too reckless. I had definitely needed time to recover.

And recover I had. A few months into 2017, the Brave Wilderness team and I began planning our return to Costa Rica, where we would film me going forearm-to-stinger with the warrior wasp. Believe it or not, part of me was excited to face the challenge. I'd endured so many venomous stings before, I wasn't even nervous. The Coyote Pack was calling, and I was ready to answer!

Mark, Mario, and I thought that the easiest way to find a warrior wasp's nest was to start with our good friend Brian. We sent a few photos to him one day, then called him up.

"Have you ever seen a wasp on your property that looks like what we sent you?" I asked. "Or, if you haven't seen the actual wasp, have you at least seen this kind of nest?"

"I'm sorry, Coyote," Brian answered. "I haven't personally, but I can ask one of the guys I work with."

Like I said in the previous chapter, Brian lives and works on over a hundred acres of densely forested

land in northeastern Costa Rica, and he hires local workers to manicure the network of trails he has on his property. Using machetes, these men face hundreds of biological land mines—like bullet ants and fer-de-lance vipers, which are some of the most dangerous snakes in the region—when they trim back trees, cut thorn bushes, and chop down limbs and vines that might snag an unsuspecting pedestrian. A man named Maximo was one of his most trusted workers, and when Brian asked him about warrior wasps, Maximo had news to share.

"There's a warrior wasp nest near the cow pasture on the far side of the property," he said excitedly. "It's way up in a tree, but it's there. I saw wasps flying into it just the other day."

Brian wanted to see the hive for himself, so the next day, he and Maximo took a 4-wheel drive vehicle across the sanctuary to check it out. I also wanted to be one hundred percent sure that this particular nest belonged to the ferocious insect I was

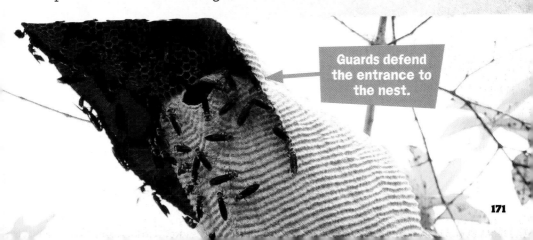

Guards defend the entrance to the nest.

looking for, so I asked my friends to snap a few photos.

"Please be careful," I said. "These wasps will swarm you!"

As the two men approached the nest, camera in hand, they threw a rock to try to entice one or two wasps to fly out. I don't know if the rock hit the tree the nest was wrapped around, or if it landed square on the hive. All I know is that, suddenly the furious wasps sensed a threat, and an onslaught of them spilled out! With a swarm of angry insects behind them, Brian and Maximo ran back to their truck as fast as they could, each getting stung a few times on the way. When they leaped into the car, panting, terrified, and on fire from the stings, they slammed their doors.

"It was insane, Coyote," Brian said breathlessly. "The wasps started dive-bombing the side of my car."

"What were the stings like?" I asked.

"Ghastly," Brian answered. "Some of the worst pain of my life."

Brian had confirmed just what I suspected; the warrior wasp sting—which Justin Schmidt described

DID YOU KNOW?
Warrior wasp nests have two access points. Once the nest has been built, the workers use pheromones to designate one access point as an entrance and the other as an exit.

as "torture...like being chained in the flow of an active volcano"—was going to be epic!

Luckily, Brian and Maximo had managed to get a few photos of the nest before they were swarmed, and I confirmed that it did, indeed, belong to a colony of warrior wasps. Like the insect who builds them, the nests are unmistakable and quite distinctive. Their impressive mass is built directly on the face of a rock or tree and is often wrapped around something like a branch. They're covered with what looks like a single sheet of grayish paper, ribbed or corrugated like the hide of an armadillo. In fact, warrior wasps are often called armadillo wasps for that very reason. In

In each hive there are 200 to 1,400 cells containing larvae.

each hive there are 200 to 1,400 cells containing larva, and unlike many types of wasps, there are several queens found in each colony.

The hive has one entrance hole at the top, and when a perceived invader approaches, the thirty or so worker wasps that hover on the outside of the hive begin pounding their wings together. In unison, they produce a distinctive *bum-bum, bum-bum, bum-bum* sound, like the march of soldiers' boots as they head into battle. This is how the insect gets its name. If someone or something then disturbs the nest—such as throwing a rock at it—the whole nest explodes, and the colony pours out in attack mode.

They point their abdomens up in the air, spread their long wings, and soar like attack helicopters toward their enemy. Then they sting en masse until the victim has retreated far enough away to no longer pose a threat to the nest, or succumbs to the stings and ultimately dies.

As you can see, these are very aggressive insects, and that's why when I drove onto Brian's property in the summer of 2017, I was both exceedingly cautious and fully prepared. Unlike all the other stinging episodes I'd filmed, I brought along a bee suit, with a hat, mask, and gloves for full coverage of my entire body. I knew that the greatest danger these wasps

Although cautious, I am fully prepared to meet the warrior wasp.

posed wasn't necessarily how painful they were, but that they could sting as a group. I had to devise a method to extract just a single specimen without causing the nest to erupt. In fact, if I did disturb the nest, I worried I might get stung through the bee suit!

Even though Maximo and his colleagues had done an amazing job clearing a path to the warrior wasp nest, it was still a two-and-a-half-mile hike from where we planned to film, and we were going to have to tromp through thick mud and extensive leaf cover. It was going to be a long, tiring day, culminating in the last horrific sting I'd ever deliberately endure.

A good distance from the wasps' nest, which was high up in a tree and wrapped around a thick branch, Mark and Mario had hung a mosquito net from the low-hanging branches of an adjacent tree. Their plan was to film me extracting a wasp from a safe distance, but if a swarm erupted from the nest, their position would allow them enough time to quickly close the mosquito net to stay protected. As I slipped into my bee suit and prepared to approach the nest, I began to

Even if they swarm, you guys stay in the net!

think about the dangerous situation I was voluntarily walking into.

I've been through so many stings, I thought, *that I'm not worried about taking a single sting. But a swarm? That's another story. Multiple stings have the potential to initiate an allergic reaction and with that, the possibility of death!*

With nervous hands, I strapped a GoPro on to the entomology net I was carrying and placed another one strategically atop my shoulder to capture the action from a first-person perspective.

Then I turned to the crew and confirmed what we'd do if a disasterous swarm struck.

"If the nest explodes with angry wasps, you guys shouldn't move," I told them. "Stay in the mosquito net and close it up tightly. The wasps won't be able to get through it."

This was it. Time to catch—or should I say, attempt to catch—a warrior wasp. Hesitantly, I left behind Mark and Mario as I began walking toward the nest. I approached cautiously,

careful not to make any sudden movements or noises that may instigate an attack. Once I reached the base of the tree and looked up, I was able to see the nest clearly for the first time. It was an impressive work of natural art.

The few dozen wasps who guarded the exterior were obviously aware of my presence. Their wings perked up, their movements calculated and poised for an attack as I slowly extended the entomology net in an attempt to coax one off the nest and into the air.

The steady drumbeat of the wasps' wings rang through the air, but much to my relief, the insects weren't overly aggressive. As the obscure, yet nonthreatening shape of the net slowly came closer to the nest, one wasp dropped from its perch in what appeared to be an exploratory mission. I took quick advantage of the moment and with a ninja-like swoop of the net...*whoosh!* I'd caught a warrior wasp!

I quickly and calmly slunk back to Mark and Mario's camp, where I dropped to the ground and looked in the net to analyze my catch. We all cheered in excitement because, sure enough, we had a perfect, unharmed specimen!

Time to take this little critter out of the net, I said to myself.

With its relatively small size, needle-thin connection between the abdomen and thorax, and papery wings, the warrior wasp appeared incredibly delicate. Even though I knew the exoskeleton was hard, I needed to be as gentle as possible. The long wings, which extended past the length of her body, had to be in the proper position when I reached into the net for extraction, so they would not be damaged. When the moment was right, I reached in with my entomology forceps and carefully grabbed hold at the back of the thorax. Then I pulled the wasp out of the net and transferred her to my trusty red-topped bouillon cube container.

We hiked the two-and-a-half miles back to our base camp—the same spot where we'd filmed the bullet ant episode—and got to work. The rain forest presents an ideal environment for filming: There's constant haze from all the humidity that acts as a natural

diffuser for the sun, eliminating harsh, stark shadows. This was lining up to be an awesome episode. The conditions for filming were in our favor, and we had the perfect specimen. All we had to do then was film the climactic ending, the moment the Coyote Pack had been waiting for: the sting!

I carefully removed the wasp from the bouillon container and transferred her into a small glass capsule, the same containment unit I'd used for several of our iconic sting episodes. Every time I film with an insect, I pay close attention to the creature when it's trapped beneath glass to study its intelligence. Is it a problem-solver? Is it angry? Is it conserving its energy? It was hard to tell what was going through the mind of the warrior wasp. She carefully climbed up the glass, exactly as she had on the surface of its hive, and inspected her alien environment. I watched as the animal systematically surveyed her surroundings, looking for an escape route. Once she realized that an immediate escape was not possible, she returned to the wooden basin and waited, almost as if knowing that eventually this glass cover would be lifted.

When the cameras started rolling, I explained my strategy: First I would move the wasp from the glass capsule into the net. Then I would carefully grasp her from the net with my trusty entomology forceps, and lastly I would place her on my forearm to induce a sting. I was ready to be stung by the most painful stinging wasp in the world! But would it be more painful than the bullet ant? I had no idea....

I took a deep breath and started speaking. "I'm Coyote Peterson, and I'm about to enter the Sting Zone with...the warrior wasp."

I counted from one to three and placed the wasp against my arm. I watched her struggle to move her abdomen as her mandibles chomped down on my skin. I slightly repositioned the insect so she could get better purchase, and seven seconds in...*wham!*...I was stung by the warrior wasp!

The pain was immediate, but rather than a searing burn, as I'd had with the bullet ant, this was a pulsing,

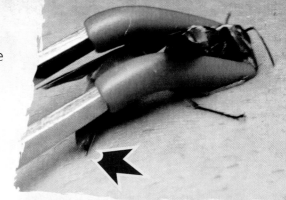

electrical pain. It was me sticking my finger in a socket rather than a fire. My forearm tingled and jolted, as if I'd been shocked, then tightened up as redness and swelling quickly set in. It felt as if as an electrical current was radiating up and down my arm in waves.

I felt faint in the minutes after I got stung, and for a few hours, my arm was red and swollen up to my elbow, with a massive welt at the site of the sting. But, like I said before, honesty is the best policy in all things. I will not lie to the Coyote Pack! Although my arm *appeared* to be in bad shape, the warrior wasp sting simply wasn't *that* bad. I'm sure if you got swarmed—as Brian and Maximo did—the stings would be sheer torture, and if your body took on enough venom, death could be possible. But from only a single sting, I didn't suffer too much. If there were a few disappointed viewers who wanted

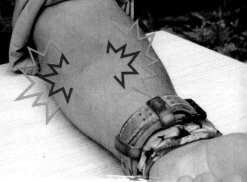

this sting to top the bullet ant episode, all I can say is that the sequel is never as good as the original, is it?

When the warrior wasp episode was released on YouTube in the fall of 2017, it hit with heavy anticipation and immediately collected millions of views. The episode even managed to become the number one trending video in the world, where it stayed for nearly twenty-four hours. While the actual sting wasn't quite as dramatic or painful as some of the others I've faced, the success of this episode can't be overlooked. What it failed to deliver as a sequel didn't seem to matter that much to the Coyote Pack  because returning to Costa Rica to film set up the next and final installment of my sting challenges.

Just as we had finished filming the warrior wasp episode, Brian informed us that he found a wasp

The warrior wasp sting was painful, but didn't dethrone the bullet ant!

species on his property that we might be interested in checking out—one that would change the course of my life and the Brave Wilderness channel forever.

This is the moment you have all been waiting for. I was about to meet the ultimate King of Sting....

The one and only...

EXECUTIONER WASP!

CHAPTER 11

THE KING OF STING!

EXECUTIONER WASP
(POLISTES CARNIFEX)

PAIN INDEX
4

You never know what challenges may lie ahead of you in life. Unexpectedly, you may face moments that test your strength and willpower, disappoint you, or come dangerously close to defeating you. Or, they might prove to be happy, fulfilling experiences that teach you valuable, once-in-a-lifetime lessons. No matter what, you must take on these challenges. Don't shy away from them! You'll be a stronger, smarter person if you face up to them, embrace them, and forge ahead.

When I walked back to my jungle hut deep in the Costa Rican rain forest after my encounter with the warrior wasp, I thought my path was clear: I was going to pack up, fly home, and never get voluntarily stung by an insect again. The Brave Wilderness crew and I would continue to travel to the most remote, wild corners of the planet, meeting all kinds of little-known creatures that would teach our viewers about conservation and respect for the marvelous animal kingdom. But, no more intentional insect stings!

Then, before I'd even rested my head on my pillow

the night of the warrior wasp encounter, life threw me a curveball....

"How did filming the sting go?" Brian asked Mark, Mario, and me as we stepped inside the cabin and started to put our equipment down.

"It was great," I answered. "The sting wasn't too bad, either. My arm is a little swollen and irritated, but I'm definitely going to be okay."

"That's great!" Brian said, "But I've got this other wasp on the property that I think you might want to look at." Although tired, in pain, and relieved to have taken my last intentional sting, Brian's enthusiasm piqued my interest. What *other wasp* could he be referring to? Part of me didn't really want to know, but as I never shy away from a challenge, I let my curiosity get the better of me. I'm a born explorer who loves nothing more than the opportunity to discover something new, so I asked him to explain.

"There are some big wasps that have built a nest up in a pavilion near that hillside over there," Brian said, pointing off into the distance. "I was weed-whacking

DID YOU KNOW?

Executioner wasps maintain relatively small nest populations, with colonies rarely exceeding fifty members.

the other day, and I got stung by one...the most painful sting I have ever felt!"

"More painful than a *bullet ant*?!" I quickly asked.

"I'd say so. I'm no entomologist, but it was a heck of

a sting, and the wasp's venom cooked a hole in my arm!"

He held out his arm and, sure enough, Brian had what appeared to be a one-centimeter round, swollen puncture wound that surrounded a small area of nearly black flesh. The inside of the divot was deep and red, like a scab that had been ripped off. It looked like a small gunshot wound, but, of course, it wasn't; my friend had been injected with a potent venom that had burned his flesh from the inside out. Brian had clearly come skin-to-stinger with an insect whose brutal sting possibly rivaled even the bullet ant! Was I going turn my back and say, *Thanks, but no thanks*? No way! I had no choice but to check out this new, unexpected force of nature.

Before I knew it, Brian was leading me and the crew up the hill he'd pointed toward, and after a short walk we arrived at a small villa next to a dry swimming pool. Nestled high in the structure's eaves was a small wasp nest that was about the size of a single head of cauliflower. It was much smaller than I imagined and appeared to be only partially built. Unlike the warrior wasp's nest, it was open, revealing about ten or so cells, some of which contained squirming white larvae.

On the hive's surface were two of the most spectacular-looking wasps I'd ever seen. They were slightly smaller than tarantula hawks—probably two inches in length—but still an incredible size for a paper wasp. They looked like a tarantula hawk-hornet hybrid, and with bright-yellow and reddish bands alternating around the length of their abdomens, they flashed with warnings of danger. Their light-brown eyes were intimidating, yet lifeless. They peered down at me like aliens, threatening that a foolish earthling like me had better think twice before getting any closer. From my safely calculated distance I could also make out the wasps' sharply pointed heads and their massive, chomping mandibles. Their expansive, amber wings stretched at forty-five-degree angles out from their thoraxes, like propellers poised to lift them off into the air for an immediate attack.

I cleared my throat. "That looks like the kind of wasp I would picture in my worst nightmare."

"My thoughts exactly," Brian said. "And I have no idea what they are."

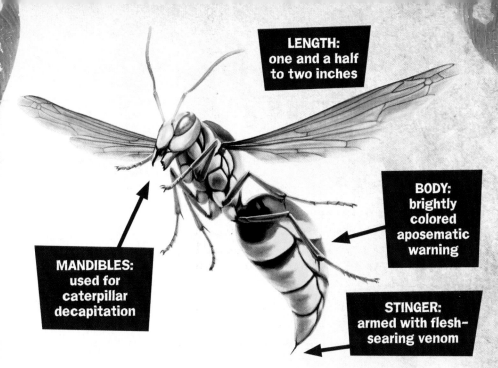

LENGTH: one and a half to two inches

BODY: brightly colored aposematic warning

MANDIBLES: used for caterpillar decapitation

STINGER: armed with flesh-searing venom

As I walked back for dinner, I felt like I'd been blindsided. One minute, Mark, Mario, and I had been celebrating the completion of the warrior wasp sting, signaling an end to deliberate stings! Now we were considering filming me getting stung again—but by a totally unknown creature.

Before I embark on any adventure with an animal— especially a stinging insect—I always do my research. So of course, later that evening, Mario and I combed through Justin Schmidt's book *Sting of the Wild*, and pored over his insect sting pain index. The extraterrestrial, flesh-burning beast that I'd seen that day was nowhere to be found. So Mario spent what felt like half the night searching websites for tropical paper wasps, and finally, in the wee hours of the morning, he landed on one website that illuminated some clues.

"I searched for the physical characteristics, hive, and location of this thing, and I can only find one article on the internet that gives me any idea as to what it is," he said. "Here's the article: 'Vespid Wasps of Latin America.'"

"What's the insect's name?" I asked, scanning the article.

Mario's eyes grew wide. "You're not going to believe this," he said, "But it's called...the Executioner wasp!"

Apparently, the scientific name for this nightmarish creature we'd stumbled upon was *Polistes carnifex,* with *carnifex* translating to "the executioner." It was described to be the largest wasp in the tropical regions of Central America and into the northern part of South America. The article said it feeds its larvae small caterpillars and insects, and while it isn't particularly aggressive, its sting is unbearably, agonizingly painful—just like Brian had described.

"I'm pretty sure this is primed to be the most terrifying insect I've ever faced," I said to Mario.

"Let's go to bed and establish our plan in the morning."

The next day, the crew and I woke up and began discussing our approach to the day over breakfast. It took some careful deliberation, but ultimately I felt I was mentally prepared to get stung again, and I was fairly confident that my body wouldn't experience any severe adverse reactions so soon after the warrior wasp sting. After all, the Brave Wilderness channel

Was I really going to catch the Executioner wasp?

is all about tackling exciting challenges, and what bigger adventure was there than being the first person to be filmed getting stung by an exotic, little-known tropical insect? Not only was there an exciting opportunity in front of me—I had a mission! Thus, the decision was made: Coyote Peterson was going to take on the Executioner wasp!

A few hours later, Mark, Mario, and I packed up our equipment and walked back toward the hill I'd summited just the day before. I briefly considered wearing my bee suit, but my research had confirmed

that I shouldn't be swarmed. Plus, I'd seen only two wasps—not dozens, like when I had faced the warrior wasp.

We were delighted to find that those two wasps—or, at least, ones that looked a heck of a lot like them—were still there, milling around on the outside of the honeycomb-shaped nest. I approached cautiously and noticed how the wasps hovered over the larvae-filled cells, protecting them. Inside those cells, though, was one of the creepiest things I'd ever seen: The larvae were pulsing, *nia-nia-nia,* like alien eggs in a science-fiction movie. I backed away slowly, then suddenly one of the wasps propped up her wings in an aggressive pose. We braced for an attack, yet, interestingly enough, the wasp held her ground.

DID YOU KNOW?

Female Executioner wasps are capable of overwintering or hibernating. Only the largest females survive the winter and start new colonies each spring.

"Woah, that was close," I said. I felt slightly panicked after seeing the monstrous wasp ready herself into striking position, but I quickly regained composure.

In the face of any challenge, you must stay absolutely focused. Even though I knew this might be the most painful experience of my life, I controlled the thought and pushed it out of my mind. I was not to be deterred. If anyone could capture wasps that could be mistaken for science-fiction creatures, it was me! I reached for my entomology net and walked toward the nest. I noticed again how robust the Executioner wasps appeared, with their thick thoraxes, large tarantula-hawkish heads, and expansive wings. I could only imagine that if you were trouncing through the jungle and one of these wasps flew past you, you would do anything you could to avoid getting in her way.

With the cameras rolling, I quietly crept closer, looking to establish the best position to execute the swing of my net. My goal was to use my extendable camera pole to gently coax a wasp from the nest and then attempt the catch. I inched closer, beads of sweat running down the side of my face as the wasps peered down with their beady eyes. In a defensive display, the outer wasp flared up her wings once more—the final warning sign they will give before charging their aggressor. Worrying that another step closer may provoke the wasp from her perch, I clenched the net with my hand, preparing for a confrontation. However, much to my surprise, as I reached up toward the giant insect, she walked right on to my camera

pole, allowing me to gently bring her down in front of the cameras. This was simply unbelievable! Without wasting the opportunity, I quickly cloaked the wasp with my net.

I had captured the Executioner wasp!

I situated myself on the ground and lay the net out flat, making sure the wasp wasn't tangled. Then, just like I had done with the warrior wasp, I opened the net slowly and gently ushered the wasp into a plastic containment capsule. I carefully stood up, grasping the catch in my hand. I was ready to head back to our jungle film set. It was time to take a sting from the Executioner!

That is one fierce-looking wasp!

Just as we had done twenty-four hours before, we trudged through the jungle back to the table where we had filmed the warrior wasp. I laid out all the elements I needed: an EpiPen, my green forceps, and the same glass container I'd used the day before. We set up the scene, transferred the insect from the containment capsule to the glass, and then sat back to admire the amazing features of this intimidating insect. At first she was flying around the capsule just like the tarantula hawk had, but after a few moments of searching for an escape route, the wasp sat at the bottom on the wooden base. She looked back at us peering in on her, a warning in her eyes: *You had better let me go, or else!*

Apparently, this calm demeanor was just a front. As soon as I transferred the wasp back to the entomology net, her aggression rose to new levels. I finally secured the perfect hold on her thorax, just behind the wings. I then gently removed her from the confines of the net and revealed her to the cameras.

This insect has a very rigid exoskeleton, and unlike the warrior wasp, she didn't feel delicate. I had to exert a surprising amount of pressure on the forceps just to keep the insect from clawing free. She was kicking her legs in all directions, and her

huge mandibles were gnashing and pinching almost constantly. This aggressive wasp wanted nothing more than to sting Coyote Peterson!

As I lowered the Executioner wasp toward my waiting forearm, we could see her massive stinger flexing in and out of her abdomen. For a wasp this size, her stinger was gigantic! It dwarfed the stinger of the bullet ant, so I knew this was going to be bad. I can't imagine a time I've been more intimidated in my life.

I held the wasp over my arm and, for the first time since I'd been stung by the bullet ant almost a full year before, I had a moment of hesitation. This sting had yet to be recorded in literature or on video—even Justin Schmidt hasn't been stung by this one! Was there a reason I was not aware of? What if the Executioner kills me? I had to make my choice. Place the wasp on my arm and take a sting, or relax my grip on the forceps and let her fly away. *Deep breaths, Coyote. The pack is watching.... here goes nothing...*

Deep breaths, Coyote. Here goes.

I looked at the camera, mustered my courage, and delivered the line everyone was waiting to hear: "I'm Coyote Peterson, and I'm about to enter the Sting Zone with...the Executioner wasp!"

With my adrenaline surging, I placed the wasp to my arm. The insect squirmed and shuddered, and finally positioned herself and swung her abdomen down. Before I could even process what was happening...

BOOM! I'd been stung!

I recall the first sensation I had was the stinger plunging deeper into my arm than any sting I'd experienced before. Sure, the velvet ant's stinger was longer, but that one went in at an angle; the Executioner's dug straight down and much deeper. Then, almost as quickly as the stinger sunk in, the venom began to take hold, and the pain hit me like a ton of bricks. It was worse than I ever imagined it would be. It felt like a grenade of lightning bolts exploded inside my forearm. Like the wasps I'd confronted before,

AGHHHHHHH!

the pain was electrifying, but I also felt the familiar singe of burning that was similar to the ant stings I had experienced in the past. This combination was stronger and more explosive than any sting or venom I'd ever felt, and it was quickly getting worse!

I dropped the forceps and quickly trapped the wasp under the glass. *"Aghhhhhhh!"* I screamed in agony as I stood up from the table. I began pacing back and forth, trying to process the overwhelming pain surging up the length of my arm.

I barely remember what happened next. My memory is only a few snapshots, but I know I fell to the ground, my hat flying off my head, and began pounding my fist into the muddy jungle floor. I recall feeling the cold, slimy sensation of my hand sinking into the saturated earth, and I screamed as my face turned beet red. The electric pain was relentless, sending stars and sparks into my brain and down my spine, rendering me lightheaded and dazed. This was the tarantula hawk times ten!

This is the tarantula hawk times ten!

We have a new King of Sting, folks. The Executioner is King!

The same intense degree of pain didn't let up for the next thirty minutes. If anything, it felt as though the pain was steadily getting stronger and stronger, pulsating with wave after agonizing wave. Honestly, it was the most consistent torture from an insect sting I'd ever felt in my life. The venom was literally burning the inside of my arm, and I feared I'd never feel relief.

Finally, after forty-five agonizing minutes, my arm started to cool. As the clouds in my head began to clear, I stood up, caked in mud, and stumbled back to the table to deliver my outro to the episode. Mark and Mario had to help me on the hike from the filming set back to our jungle hut, which was an hour through heat and humidity. I was sweaty, delirious, and unsteady the entire way. This was one of the hardest walks through a jungle I'd ever endured.

On arriving back at base camp, I noticed that my forearm had swollen nearly as much as it had with the bullet ant sting, and the sting zone was bright red. The spot where the wasp pierced my skin was indented deep into my flesh and looked as though I

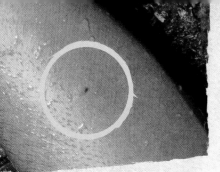

had been jabbed with a thick-gauge needle. I glanced over at the Executioner wasp safely secured in the containment capsule, knowing that this insect was going to be a star. Even though my arm was wracked with pain and my head still felt hazy, I held nothing but admiration for this beastly insect. Seeing her probe the capsule for an escape route reminded me that it was time to set her free, and in my state of delirium I slogged through the trail and back to the eaves where I had caught her.

The swelling continued to grow until my arm looked like a water balloon, and for the next thirty-six hours, I faced waves of intense pain. Within a week, the venom had cooked a hole in my arm, and a divot formed like a freshly picked chicken pox scab. The flesh around the wound was sensitive and raw, which means the venom had broken down my skin cells, causing my flesh to deteriorate. The sore was painful and disgusting, but I diligently prevented it from getting infected by constantly keeping it clean.

The insect sting pain index ranks specimens from one through four, and I can say without question that the Executioner wasp is a four. This proudly puts it in the ranks of the tarantula hawk, warrior wasp, and bullet ant; however, in my opinion this giant paper wasp truly stands at the top of sting mountain. Just a single sting combined all the traits these other insects' stings possess, but none of them—not even the bullet ant—seared a hole in my arm.

Imagine, for a moment, being attacked by a swarm of angry Executioner wasps. Not only are they able to fly, but they are also able to follow. You can outrun an exploding nest of ground-dwelling bullet ants; you can avoid a single tarantula hawk; and, no matter how many warrior wasp stings you may endure, their venom is not capable of destroying flesh. So, when you place these four insects in a lineup, it's easy to see why I have defined the Executioner wasp as the rightful King of Sting.

As I write this book a year later, the hole in my forearm is gone, but I still have a faint scar that serves as a constant reminder of the time I went skin-to-stinger with the Executioner wasp. What's

more exciting is that, as I
finish this chapter, the video
you have all been waiting
for is also finishing its journey
through postproduction. Boy, is
it a wonder to behold.

I can't predict how the video will perform when it's
released on YouTube in the winter of 2018, but after
everything my team and I went through to produce
it, I can't wait to see how the Coyote Pack responds.
I don't think there has ever been a video in YouTube
history that has been more highly anticipated than
"STUNG by an Executioner Wasp!" And for that I
can thank the members of the Coyote Pack, who
have cheered me on and waited patiently for the
episode's release. I hope you all enjoy it as much as
we have enjoyed bringing you this unique education
into the world of stinging insects.

THE SUMMIT

After enduring the agony of the Executioner wasp
sting, I truly felt as if I had reached the summit of sting
mountain. Is there a sting out there in the world that
is more painful? Perhaps there is a wasp waiting to be
discovered in a far-off, sweltering jungle. Or maybe
a unique ant species roaming in a desolate desert.
I'd say, possibly. No...probably. But it won't be Coyote
Peterson who is willing to get stung by it for science and
entertainment.

The Brave Wilderness YouTube channel has
enjoyed an incredible amount of success stemming
from my ability to brave a multitude of insect stings.
In fact, you could go as far as to say the success is
unprecedented. To date, the channel has over twelve
million subscribers and boasts more than two billion

views, making Brave Wilderness one of the fastest-growing channels in YouTube history, and the world's largest animal adventure brand in the digital space. Yet the statistic that is most important to us is that in the process of this chaos, we have helped *countless people* understand and appreciate creepy crawlies.

So while I may have closed the door on intentionally getting stung by venomous insects, my work in the world of animals is far from over. Sometimes it feels as if the journey has just begun. As I look back on the four years we have traveled thus far, I see the ever-growing family that is our Coyote Pack. Thank you, to each and every member, because without your love and excitement for the natural world, the Brave Wilderness crew and I would not stand where we are today. There are still many fascinating animals we dream to encounter, and the journeys we have yet to embark upon are just a new set of mountains that we are excited to climb.

Be Brave...Stay Wild, and we'll see you on the next adventure!